THE
COUNSELOR'S GUIDE

to
Learning
To Live
Without
Violence

Daniel Jay Sonkin, Ph.D.

**Preface by
Donald G. Dutton, Ph.D.**

Volcano, CA

First printing, Volcano Press, Inc., 1995
Printed in the United States of America.

Library of Congress Cataloging-in-Publication Data

Sonkin, Daniel Jay.
    The counselor's guide to learning to live without violence / by
Daniel Jay Sonkin.
        p.   cm.
    Includes bibliographical references.
    ISBN 1-884244-03-3 : $29.95
    1. Abusive men—Counseling of. 2. Wife abuse—Prevention.
I. Sonkin, Daniel Jay. Learning to live without violence. II. Title.
RC569.5.F3S66   1994
616.85'822—dc20   94-34683
                                                                           CIP

Cover and text design by David Charlsen
Typesetting by Jeffrey Brandenburg/ImageComp
Edited by Zoe Brown

Please enclose $29.95 for each copy ordered. For postage and handling, add $4.50 for the first book ordered, and $1.00 for each additional book. California residents please add appropriate sales tax. Please contact Volcano Press for quantity discount prices, and for a free catalog.

Volcano Press
P.O. Box 270 SDV   (800) 879-9636
Volcano, CA 95689   FAX (209) 296-4995

See order form at the end of this book for additional titles on the subject of domestic violence from Volcano Press.

To Marissa,
who holds the potential for a more compassionate
world in her spirit and soul.

ACKNOWLEDGMENTS

Over the past eighteen years I have met many women and men who have helped me grow both professionally and personally. Most importantly, Michael Durphy, Don Dutton, Del Martin, Michael Searle and Lenore Walker have all been and continue to be sources of inspiration and support. Likewise, there have been countless women and men activists and mental health professionals I have met across the country and around the world who are heroines and heroes in their own communities. I have learned much from their creative efforts to assist battered women, children and perpetrators to realize their dreams and live a life without violence. Additionally, I have a great deal of respect and appreciation for the many researchers who have struggled to understand the issues of domestic violence. These individuals have made it more and more possible for clinicians, like myself, to integrate their research findings into psychoeducational approaches to treating male batterers.

I would like to also thank my publisher, Ruth Gottstein, for having the courage and foresight to take my first book, *Learning to Live without Violence*, and add it to her all-woman author list of excellent titles. Her ongoing support over the past fifteen years has made the difficult task of writing a lot easier. I would also like to thank the entire staff at Volcano Press. Likewise, I would like to thank my editors, David Charlsen and Zoe Brown, for the way they transformed the manuscript from a rough first draft to a book that I can be proud of.

I would like to thank the many men and women who have entrusted their lives to me in my clinical practice over the years. They have shared their most private thoughts, feelings and experiences and in doing so have taught me about the human capacity to rise above despair and find hope and new meaning in life. Through them I have learned as much about myself as I have about this issue.

Lastly, I would like to thank my wife and life partner, Mindy Rosenberg, who has always supported and encouraged my desires to write. Her professionalism, knowledge and creative ideas have inspired me to stretch beyond my reach so that I can write a book that has far exceeded my expectations. Her love is a constant source of strength and it continues to remind me that, as John Lennon wrote, in the end the love you take is equal to the love you make. Thank you.

CONTENTS

Preface . . . . **vii**

Introduction . . . . **ix**

1. Treatment of Male Batterers: No Easy Answers **1**

2. What Is Violence? **15**

3. What Counseling Approach Should I Use? **31**

4. The Assessment Process **47**

5. Using *Learning to Live without Violence:* An Introduction . . **69**

6. Cognitive and Behavioral Interventions **87**

7. Crises and Dangerous Situations **103**

8. Interventions with Couples **117**

9. Cross-cultural Issues **133**

10. A Stalking Prevention Program **149**

Epilogue: A Final Word to the Reader **163**

Suggested Reading **169**

PREFACE

Treatment groups for assaultive men began in the late 1970s as one response to a growing public awareness of the problem of wife assault. Daniel Sonkin pioneered the development of treatment groups at that time, and his profile of batterers in his co-edited book, *The Male Batterer,* stands up well to the test of time, as does his other book, *Domestic Violence on Trial,* which was ahead of its time in examining court-related issues in domestic violence. His original workbook, *Learning to Live without Violence,* has been widely used as a source of anger-management exercises. For years, however, a good manual that addresses the multitude of issues confronting counselors treating violent men has been missing.

As someone who has personally run treatment groups for batterers for sixteen years, I would have loved to have had the present manual when I started. Even now, it's a pleasure to see the clear and even treatment of the sometimes convoluted issues of batterer treatment handled as adroitly as Daniel Sonkin has done in this manual.

Beginning with an historical overview and a lucid description of treatment issues, Daniel moves through a thorough definition of the problem, choices of counseling approaches, and assessment. Then, turning his attention to cognitive-behavioral approaches, he clearly outlines a user-friendly guide to group treatment. Violent men pose lethality risks for their spouses, and Daniel wisely includes a chapter on risk assessment and management. He concludes with three related chapters on couples therapy, cross-cultural issues, and stalking prevention that nicely round out a very comprehensive introduction for the professional reader.

Treatment groups have received some criticism, not all of it justified. It has been said that they "don't work," or that they "only work for those who are motivated." Certainly, a therapeutic trick in running court-mandated treatment groups is to find ways of building and maintaining the men's motivation. I like to think of the process of change from violence in the terms described by James Prochaska and his colleagues in the *American Psychologist* in 1992. They describe

five stages to the change process from precontemplation to mainte-
nance. They see it as a spiral process that proceeds nonlinearly. However, when men do complete treatment they are less likely to reoffend.
Those who had completed the group were tracked for eleven years,
and we found that compared to the dropouts their recidivism rate
was halved. Of course, they had better motivation, but that motivation led them to apply the skills taught in this book. Daniel Sonkin
has applied his breadth and clarity in sharing the processes through
which you can impart those skills.

Donald G. Dutton, Ph.D.
Department of Psychology, University of British Columbia
Author of *The Domestic Assault of Women*

INTRODUCTION

Learning to Live without Violence: A Handbook for Men was first published twelve years ago when the vast majority of materials available on the issue of domestic violence were directed towards victims, and rightfully so — it was the victims whose lives were in constant danger and needing shelter, criminal justice protection, and counseling. Descriptions of male batterers came primarily from interviews with battered women. At the time, there were only a few programs across the country specifically geared towards counseling men. Programs like EMERGE in Boston and Anne Ganley and Lance Harris's program at American Lakes Veterans Hospital in Tacoma, Washington, began to set the tone for programs throughout the United States as well as abroad. Although these early programs each had their own individual differences in the way they counseled spouse abusers, there were also many similarities in their approaches. They were all programs committed to stopping marital violence by using behavioral techniques in conjunction with education about sex-role socialization and how it contributes to violence against women. At that time, however, much of what we knew and espoused about the male batterer came from clinical observations as opposed to empirical data.

By the mid-1980s, interested professionals who were affiliated with academic institutions were beginning to study this issue. Clinical and political theories were soon to be augmented by empirical data. Academic researchers have greatly contributed to our understanding of the male batterer. Yet we still have not reached any definitive answers as to what causes men to become violent and how to best address this issue clinically.

Meanwhile, great strides have been made by advocates for battered women in bringing about changes to the response of the criminal justice system to domestic violence The general public's awareness of this issue has been raised as well. Yet even as I write, the newspapers are full of stories regarding family violence and domestic homicide. This has particularly been brought to our awareness with the recent arrest and trial of famed football star O.J. Simpson for the murder of his ex-wife and her male friend.

Although theories abound, little is really known about why some men use violence and the majority do not. Yet the numbers of cases of domestic violence are not simply a small group of aberrant individuals. It is estimated that approximately two million women experience at least one episode of severe domestic violence each year. *Severe* is defined as punching, kicking, choking, beatings, threats with a knife or gun, or having a knife or gun used on them. If pushing and shoving were included in this definition, the numbers of abused women would be even more staggering. Yet violence against the partner is not the only problem that families experience. Child abuse and alcohol/drug abuse both occur at similarly high rates, and both the clinical and research data suggest that these problems are not separate and distinct but somehow related. The majority of male batterers has experienced some form of child maltreatment in the past or simultaneously abuse alcohol or drugs. The exact relationship between these problems is yet to be clarified, but researchers have begun to tackle this issue in the study of male batterers.

With so little understood about this population, how can we write a book about treatment of male batterers that will stand the test of time? Unlike other medical fields where our knowledge is changing almost daily, such as the treatment of diseases such as HIV, the study of human behavior is a slowly evolving field where changes develop over time rather than overnight. This book provides an overview of the treatment of male batterers. It also provides specific directions and information for working with *Learning to Live without Violence: A Handbook for Men*. The Learning to Live without Violence Program is partly based on the empirical literature and partly based on my own experience of what works for the men I have treated. This approach has its strengths and limitations. Some activists and counselors may disagree with my theoretical orientation, assumptions, or proposed interventions in counseling male batterers. However, given the wide variety of men who experience violence, it is my firm belief that until the research shows otherwise, there is much room for different ways to approach the issue of counseling male batterers.

This counseling guide was primarily written to stimulate thought, suggest specific methods of intervention, expand horizons, and most importantly, encourage creativity and thoughtfulness in developing a theoretical perspective for the counseling of male batterers. Additionally, it was written for the thousands of counselors who have used *Learning to Live without Violence* over the past twelve years and have found it to be a valuable resource in their work with male batterers. Thank you for your support, and I hope you also find this book helpful in your work in ending domestic violence.

A final note of caution: Because of the potential high lethality inherent in dealing with domestic violence cases, this book should be used only by licensed mental health professionals, criminal justice personnel, or paraprofessionals with extensive training in the assessment and treatment of the violent individual. In addition, counselors must be knowledgeable about legal and ethical issues relating to dangerous clients. Unlicensed professionals, in particular, should understand the limits of their knowledge and experience and therefore know when to consult with trained professionals. It is encouraged that counselors working with this population receive ongoing consultation with persons knowledgeable of this client population.

CHAPTER ONE

Treatment of Male Batterers: No Easy Answers

Since the early 1970s, the issue of spouse abuse has become an increasing focus of attention for both professionals and the general public. The first book for the general public on the subject in this country, *Battered Wives* by Del Martin (1976, rev. 1981), was primarily focused on bringing the issue into the public awareness. Spouse abuse was described as a problem embedded in the fabric of society — and that changes in social policy would be necessary in developing a solution. Many controversies have surrounded this issue over the years, the first being whether or not this was a serious problem at all. Critics claimed that abuse occurred only in a very small slice of the population. On the other hand, activists claimed that as many as fifty percent of all women have been abused by their partner. Not until studies were conducted like those of Murray Straus, Richard Gelles, and Suzanne Steinmetz (1980) did we begin to see just how prevalent this problem was. Still, it has only been recently that the public has become aware of the pervasiveness of domestic violence and the need for services for victims, their children, and the perpetrators (Koss, Goodman, Fitzgerald, Russo, Keita, and Browne, 1994).

The term *spouse abuse* has also been a focus of controversy. Critics of the terms *spouse abuse, family violence,* and *domestic violence* have

1

argued that the majority of victims are women, and therefore terms such as *woman battering* and *wife abuse* more accurately describe the direction of violence. Others indicate that violence is perpetrated by both women and men and that gender-specific terminology is misleading. The chosen semantics are often a function of an individual's orientation to this issue, whether political, academic, and/or clinical.

Another disagreement has been whether we should first provide treatment for offenders, versus jail followed by treatment. Proponents of the incarceration alternative state that perpetrators must get the message that domestic violence is a crime with serious criminal justice consequences. They say that sending batterers to counseling is another way the system minimizes the seriousness of the problem. Those opposed to this point of view argue that the jails are already overcrowded, that incarceration only postpones what is ultimately needed — treatment — and that men do get the message that this is criminal behavior when they have to hire a lawyer and go to court. Another point of contention relates to whether or not battered women's shelters should provide treatment for male batterers or whether these programs should be independently run in the community. Proponents of the shelter offender programs state that having the program under the auspices of the shelter gives the women's movement greater control over how the programs are run. Opponents suggest that men's and women's programs should be separate. Shelters have enough difficulty keeping themselves funded without having to also take care of the men. And one of the most prevalent controversies relating to perpetrator treatment has to do with how treatment is conducted.

COUNSELING THE MALE BATTERER

As a result of advocacy efforts of the women's movement for the better part of this century, the problem of violence against women has become a part of the social consciousness. The issue reached the social awareness as a result of a political movement that related the phenomenon to the economic and political oppression of women.

Up until this time the mental health profession largely ignored this issue — not that it didn't surface within the context of psychotherapy. Clinical interventions with battered women often ranged from benign neglect to blaming the victim and supporting the offender.

Sociologists Suzanne Steinmetz and Murray Straus (1974) were the first behavioral scientists to address this issue. Their writing focused on the etiology of the problem and solutions on the social level. Their efforts were the beginning of the legitimization of the issue within the professional community. In the mid- to late 1970s, feminist psychologist Lenore Walker (1979) began to examine the individual psychological contingencies of the problem of wife beating. Her work also focused on translating feminist theory into clinical practice with battered women.

Simultaneously, clinical descriptions of the male batterer had begun to add to our understanding of this complex phenomenon. As early as 1977, social worker Margaret Elbow (1977) wrote descriptions of the types of male batterers (controller, defender, approval-seeker, and incorporator). This concept was quite innovative, because it wasn't until the mid-1980s that researchers began to entertain the possibility that there was no prototypic male batterer *per se* but instead subcategories of perpetrators.

Over the last fourteen years, intervention programs for the abuser have begun to proliferate across the country. These programs have grown out of the realization that stopping violent behavior rests with the offender, not the victim. In addition, public policy changes have also included the institution of mandatory arrest and pre- and post-trial diversion laws, thereby making it necessary to refer more men into treatment programs. Because of the lack of available empirical data on the domestic violence offender, many of these programs have been based on personal experience, interest, and common sense. These early pioneers had only sparse literature on domestic violence to draw from and therefore turned to other areas, such as substance abuse and criminology.

Many of the first programs for abusers were developed by individuals who were actively involved in the battered women's movement and who recognized the need for intervention with male perpetrators of violence. The treatment philosophy of these early service providers, such as EMERGE in Boston, tended to reflect their political ideologies. For this reason, early interventions for male batterers would focus on sex-role issues and power and control in intimate relationships, with particular emphasis on men taking responsibility for their behavior and immediately ceasing their violence. Many of these early programs were strongly feminist-based, and as such emphasized peer-facilitated groups — with the focus of intervention being men's violence against women, power and control in relationships, male sex-role socialization, and the program's collective model for decision-making.

Mental health professionals, such as Anne Ganley and Lance Harris (1978) at American Lakes Veterans Hospital in Tacoma, Washington, developed an inpatient program that was a highly structured, behavioral approach utilizing anger and stress management, social problem-solving skills, and the examination of personal attitudes that may have encouraged violence towards family members. Today, these early programs still stand as models for many batterers programs across the country.

When Michael Durphy and I started counseling men in groups in 1978, we attempted to integrate psychological and feminist theories into an approach that would be effective with the population of men with whom we were working. We worked in conjunction with a local battered women's shelter and the Marin County District Attorney's Office, which at that time was one of the few in the country aggressively addressing domestic violence. *Learning to Live without Violence* started out as handouts that we would give to men in the group, depending on the topic we were discussing in any particular week.

California was one of the first states to enact a Domestic Violence Diversion law, in 1980. This law required that persons arrested for acts constituting domestic violence, if they met certain criteria, were mandated into a counseling or education program from six months to two years. Many cases that would have been ordinarily dismissed by the courts were now being referred into diversion. Due to the potentially large number of diversion cases, criminal justice programs, such as the San Francisco Family Violence Project (now called the Family Violence Prevention Fund), and shelters for battered women, began to organize batterer treatment services in their respective communities. Treatment consortiums were developed, comprised of agencies and individuals from the community that were interested in offering services to male batterers. These consortiums met regularly to manage cases, discuss problems, and share information. These meetings also encouraged coordination of batterer services with shelters, criminal justice programs, alcohol and drug services, and mental health services.

As other states have enacted mandatory arrest and domestic violence diversion laws, and the issue has reached the consciousness of other mental health service providers, increasing numbers of traditional programs have begun to offer treatment services for perpetrators of family violence. As these services for offenders have proliferated over the past fourteen years, there have been greater differences in the treatment approaches offered. Although many programs still offer group services, others offer individual, couples, or family counseling. To date, no studies have indicated that any one approach or modality is more effective than others in stopping violence.

Evaluation research in this area has indicated that many batterer treatment programs have a high success rate (Dutton, 1988, rev. 1995). However, many controversial issues are still unresolved with regard to the effectiveness of different *types* of treatment programs. Some of the components involved in this debate include: 1) the content (e.g., anger management, gender/feminist analysis, and family systems, etc.) of the program; 2) the process (educational vs. therapeutic vs. consciousness-raising); 3) modality (individual, couple, family or group) of these sessions; 4) the length of treatment; and 5) to what extent the victim shares in the process of stopping violent behavior.

Although a number of evaluation studies have been conducted (Dutton, Bodnarchuk, Kropp, Hart, and Ogloff, 1994; Farley and Magill, 1988; Gondolf, 1988; Poynter, 1989), it is still unclear as to whether or not it is a *particular intervention* or an *intervention at all* that is the significant variable. Some providers continue to argue with great vehemence in support of their particular orientations with no outcome studies to support such claims that treatment "A" is more effective than treatment "B." The evaluation of the differing approaches is confounded by significant social variables. Because most programs are short-term (six months or less) it may be argued that the content, process, or modality of treatment is not as significant a variable in predicting success in treatment as are the social consequences for battering (fine, jail, or loss of spouse and/or children).

As more treatment programs are evaluated and compared to differing treatment approaches, there will need to be greater understanding as to the length of treatment exposure necessary to bring about an end of violent behaviors. The vast majority of programs has been developed as short-term interventions (six months or less). Although preliminary studies indicate that many men will greatly benefit from such programs, the offender who has a long-term pattern of violence and poor social problem-solving skills may need to keep in contact with a program for many years.

VICTIM BLAMING

One concern of advocates of battered women relates to the issue of responsibility for violent behaviors. It has been argued by feminist mental health service providers that for many years battered women have been labeled masochistic, provocative, or psychotic, and therefore have not been believed as to the seriousness of the situation by mental health professionals. This blaming of the victim made it impossible for women to receive useful assistance from the mental health profession. Such labels have only served to keep the victim in a life-threatening situation, immobilized by her own perception of inadequacy and helplessness. So for many years, battered women shelters alone provided the needed support and counseling for women until education within the mental health community led to changes in attitudes.

Blaming the victim is not a new idea to victims of physical, political, or racial violence. There has been a concern, by persons active in the field of domestic violence, that couples or family therapists may either purposefully or inadvertently give the victim the message that she is somehow responsible for her partner's violent behavior. Likewise, there is concern that even the traditionally trained individual or group therapist may also give the offender similar messages with regard to responsibility for violence. On the other hand, it is argued by systems-oriented therapists that one can utilize a couples or family modality of treatment and not overtly or covertly give such messages. Some clinicians, such as Robert Geffner at the East Texas Crisis Center, have developed treatment interventions geared toward couples (Geffner and Mantooth, 1989). He and his colleagues believe that by treating both the victims and perpetrators of violence together they are more likely to help the couple develop a more satisfying relationship without abuse, while at the same time increase self-esteem, improve communication skills, and reduce stress and hostility. Gayla Margolin at the University of Southern California has conducted extensive research on communication patterns in violent families and has found characteristics of both men and women that may contribute to increased hostility and abuse (Burman, Margolin, and John, 1993). Neidig and Friedman (1986) indicate in their rationale for couples treatment that women do contirubute to the escalation process that may lead to violence. Although the victim is not overtly blamed for the offender's violence, she is partly held accountable for the escalation of anger and conflict.

All of this controversy, however, is within the context of no empirical research that has indicated that couples therapy is any more, less, or as effective as offender-focused treatment approaches. The jury is still out in this regard. Therefore, it is suggested that counselor philosophy of treatment, with regard to this particular issue, seems to be more a reflection of personal beliefs and attitudes rather than scientific fact.

THE BATTERER PROFILE

As with the treatment issues, many professionals and paraprofessionals have made an effort to justify certain prevention and/or intervention strategies by trying to develop a "batterer profile." Early descriptions of men who assault female partners — including attributes such as use of minimization and denial as a defensive coping mechanism, externalization, conservative sex-role attitudes, lack of skills in identifying and communicating feelings, etc.— have been useful clinical tools but were not uniquely characteristic of batterers. Many of these descriptions reflect qualities seen in men with other behavior problems such as substance abuse, child abuse, and sexual assault. In fact, to one degree or another, the above qualities could be utilized to describe men in general. Therefore, from a research point of view, these characteristics do little to help us understand why some men batter and many do not.

Today, as research findings have increased our knowledge of the abuser, some clinicians and researchers have come to realize that there is not only one profile of the abuser. That there are different types of abusers is reflected in their personalities, etiologies, and the violence perpetrated. The current trend of the research is to describe the various types of batterers, based on multiple variables.

In her dissertation, P. Lynn Caesar (1985) described three groups of batterers (tyrants, rescuers exposed to violence in family of origin, and altruists not exposed to violence in family of origin). She based the categories on data from the MMPI (Minnesota Multiphasic Personality Inventory), the role of alcohol, violence in family of origin, and the relationship and violence with the wife. She also described a fourth group (psychotic/schizophrenic) based on the MMPI, history of psychiatric hospitalization, and alcohol use. Dan Saunders (1987) at the University of Wisconsin describes a theoretical model of two types of batterers (dependent and dominant) based on data including severity of violence, attitudes towards women, modes of marital decision-making, level of conflict, anger towards partner, jealousy, depression, and alcohol use. Both of these researchers have gone beyond the clinical experience and have tested their descriptions with clinical research studies. Likewise, Hastings and Hamberger (1988), using psychometric tests, found batterers to fit into four diagnostic categories (schizoidal/borderline, narcissistic/antisocial, passive dependent/compulsive, and mixed).

Criminologists Nancy Shields, George McCall, and Christine Hanneke (1988) at the Policy Research Planning Group in St. Louis, Missouri, have also contributed to our understanding of the different types of men who batter by describing three types of violent men: those who are violent only within the family, those who are violent both within and outside the family, and those who are violent only outside the family.

Don Dutton, professor of psychology at the University of British Columbia, has conducted considerable research on the male batterer, and his findings have shed great light on this problem. Dutton suggests that many male batterers may be suffering from a disorder of attachment that results in high levels of anxiety, as well as other dysphoric mood states, when involved in intimate relationships (Dutton, Saunders, Starzomski, and Bartholomew, 1994). These men regulate their mood state by adjusting closeness and distance (degrees of attachment) or by changing their environment (controlling their partner and children). Hence many male batterers withdraw from potential conflict, inappropriately intrude on personal boundaries of others, and attempt to control the perceived external cause of their discomfort. These men are so sensitive to rejection that they are likely to interpret any disagreement or uncomfortable emotional interaction as potentially threatening. Ironically, even though these men find intimacy so threatening, they are very dependent on their partner for a sense of self — that is, who they are; their value and worth are partly determined by their partner's love and acceptance. So when she leaves or wants a separation, the men find this situation very threatening and therefore anxiety-producing. Getting the partner to return is one way of managing this anxiety and is an attempt to return to wholeness.

My own clinical experience has indicated that, although there seems to be some overlap in childhood histories and motivations for and qualities of violence, there are also significant differences between clients. With this in mind, it is important that service providers maintain a degree of flexibility in their conceptualization of their method of intervention. Given the large number of men who batter and their social and psychological differences, research in the typology of male batterers appears to be a fruitful endeavor.

SICK OR SOCIALLY ASSIMILATED

The batterer's profile brings up the question, "Are we dealing with a psychological problem at all?" Some feminist-oriented programs, who define battering as a social problem, ascribe psychological interventions to misattributions that take the focus away from society and place it on the individual. Many of these feminist programs do not conduct individual or group psychotherapy; instead, they call their intervention *reeducation, education, self-help,* etc. These perspectives are not mutually exclusive. Just as with alcoholism, a social problem of probably greater magnitude, interventions are necessary on the individual level while social policy changes are occurring on the community level. Socially conscious therapists include a social perspective in their work with clients, so that the individual will better understand the relationship between his psyche and the social network.

There are many domestic violence service providers who are not professionally trained to conduct psychotherapy; however, their knowledge and understanding of domestic violence and men's consciousness-raising can be an invaluable asset to groups of men seeking alternatives to violent behavior. These paraprofessionals shouldn't let any beliefs about the social etiology of this problem deter them from making referrals for psychotherapy when appropriate. Likewise, professionally trained therapists may find their work with this population easier if they either address the social-psychological aspects of violence themselves or make collateral referrals to men's programs in their community. Only through mutual respect and consideration between service providers will we be able to adequately assist individuals as well as effect the necessary changes on the community level.

EVALUATION OF SERVICES

Changes in public policy, such as mandatory arrest and diversion laws, have had a great impact on both the professional and community levels. These changes have resulted in more arrests of male batterers, a greater number of victims leaving their abusive partners, and subsequently a greater number of men referred for treatment services. For example, as a result of mandatory arrest and diversion laws in California, many men are now being referred to treatment that ordinarily may not have availed themselves of such services. Even the self-referred or wife-referred men find the potential legal consequences sobering. The social sanctions for battering are becoming more a part of the individual's consciousness. However, as the numbers of programs and clients seeking services increase, the need for evaluation of programs becomes more pressing.

The problems inherent in evaluating treatment services for male batterers are many and complex. However, it is ethically important to determine if a client is stopping his violent behavior. Unlike most other persons who receive mental health services, male batterers pose a serious danger to others. Therefore it is necessary for service providers to determine if a client is utilizing treatment interventions so as to minimize risk to family members. Patient follow-up procedures are a common component of programs serving offenders. When evaluating effectiveness of treatment, clearly defining violence is a necessary prerequisite to accurately determining success. Many programs adopt a definition of violence, commonly accepted in this field, that includes physical, sexual, and psychological violence. A number of forms have been developed for research and/or clinical use to determine the extent of violent behaviors, such as the Violence Inventory developed by this author and the Conflict Tactics Scales developed by Murray Straus, Richard Gelles, and Suzanne Steinmetz (1980) for their survey. The Violence Inventory specifically focuses on violent acts perpetrated, whereas the Conflict Tactics Scales focus on conflict-solving strategies. Unfortunately, most clinicians either do not take the time or are unskilled at taking a comprehensive violence history. Many times they are unaware that a client is continuing to violently act out while in treatment.

In evaluating intervention outcome, clearly defined criteria for success are necessary. However, there are many differences in these standards that give rise to difficulties in comparing differing intervention strategies. Many programs will consider nonarrest as success. Others may only include severe physical violence or not include psychological violence in their evaluation of treatment outcome. Most importantly, programs must be clear as to what treatment or education goals they are trying to achieve and how those goals will be evaluated. These goals must also be articulated to referring agencies, perpetrators, and their families.

IN SUMMARY

Individuals and groups providing services to male batterers need to intermingle so that cross-fertilization can occur. No one program or person has the definitive answer to this problem. Domestic violence is a complex social and psychological phenomenon that has no easy answers. What is most evident from the domestic violence literature is that there are many committed individuals who are genuinely interested in offering solutions to the violence around us. At this point in time, however, the male batterer is still a stranger in our midst. We are just beginning to shed light on what differentiates him from nonviolent men. Much more study is necessary to thoroughly unravel this problem. As we better understand the psychology of the male batterer, we will ultimately be better prepared to develop appropriate treatment interventions and strategies. Perhaps we will discover that interventions on community, individual, and family systems levels will be necessary for the cessation of violent behaviors.

REFERENCES

Burman, Bonnie; Margolin, Gayla; and John, Richard S. (1993). America's angriest home videos: Behavioral contingencies observed in home reenactments of marital conflict. Special Section: Couples and couple therapy. *Journal of Consulting & Clinical Psychology*, Feb., v61 (n1), 28-39.

Caesar, P.L. (1985). *The male batterer: Personality and psychosocial characteristics*. Unpublished doctoral dissertation, California School of Professional Psychology, Berkeley, CA.

Dutton, D.G. (1988, rev. 1995). *The domestic assault of women: Psychological and criminal justice perspectives*. Boston: Allyn & Bacon, Inc.

Dutton, D.G.; Bodnarchuk, M.; Kropp, R.; Hart, S.; and Ogloff, J. (1994). *A ten-year follow-up of court-mandated wife assault treatment*. Vancouver, BC: British Columbia Institute of Family Violence.

Dutton, D.G.; Saunders, K.; Starzomski, A.; and Batholomew, K. (1994). Intimacy-anger and insecure attachment as precursors of abuse in intimate relationships. *Journal of Applied Social Psychology*, 24 (15), 1367-1386.

Elbow, M. (1977). Theoretical considerations of violent marriages. *Social Casework*, Oct., v63 (8), 465-471.

Farley, Dennis and Magill, Judith (1988). An evaluation of a group program for men who batter. Special Issue: Violence: Prevention and treatment in groups. *Social Work with Groups*, 11 (3), 53-65.

Ganley, A. and Harris, L. (1978). *Domestic violence: Issues in designing and implementing programs for male batterers*. Paper presented at the 86th Annual Convention of the American Psychological Association, Toronto, Canada.

Geffner, R. and Mantooth, C. (1989). A psychoeducational conjoint therapy approach to reducing family violence. In: P.L. Caesar and L.K. Hamberger (eds.), *Treating men who batter: Theory, practice and programs*. New York: Springer Publications.

Gondolf, Edward W. (1988). How some men stop their abuse: An exploratory program evaluation. In: Gerald T. Hotaling, David Finkelhor, John T. Kirkpatrick, and Murray A. Straus (eds.), *Coping with family violence: Research and policy perspectives*. Newbury Park, CA: Sage Publications, Inc., pp. 129-144.

Hastings, J. and Hamberger, L.K. (1988). Personality characteristics of spouse abusers: A controlled comparison. *Violence and Victims*, Spring, v3 (1), 31-48.

Koss, M.; Goodman, L.; Fitzgerald, L.; Russo, N.F.; Keita, G.P.; and Browne, A. (1994). *No safe haven: Male violence against women at home, at work and in the community.* Washington, DC: American Psychological Association.

Martin, Del (1976, rev. 1981). *Battered wives.* Volcano, CA: Volcano Press.

Neidig, P. and Friedman, D. (1986). *Domestic violence containment: A spouse abuse treatment program.* Urbana, IL: Research Press.

Poynter, Tracey L. (1989). An evaluation of a group programme for male perpetrators of domestic violence. *Australian Journal of Sex, Marriage & Family,* 10 (3), 133-142.

Saunders, D. (1987). *Are there three different types of men who batter? An empirical study with possible implications for treatment.* Paper presented at the Third National Family Violence Research Conference. July 6-9, Durham, New Hampshire.

Shields, N.M.; McCall, G.J.; and Hanneke, C.R. (1988). Patterns of family and nonfamily violence: Violent husbands and violent men. *Violence and Victims,* Summer, v3 (2), 83-98.

Sonkin, D.J. and Durphy, M. (1982, rev. 1989). *Learning to live without violence: A handbook for men.* Volcano, CA: Volcano Press.

Steinmetz, S.K. and Straus, M. (1974). *Violence in the family.* New York: Harper and Row.

Straus, M.A.; Gelles, R.J.; and Steinmetz, S.K. (1980). *Behind closed doors: Violence in the American family.* New York: Anchor-Doubleday.

Walker, L.E.A. (1979). *The battered woman.* New York: Harper and Row.

CHAPTER TWO

What Is Violence?

Developing a working definition of domestic violence is an important first step to identifying those behaviors the program is designed to stop. Domestic violence consists of physical, sexual, and psychological violence perpetrated by an individual in an intimate relationship. This relationship may be dating or committed as manifested by cohabitation or marriage. The ages of these individuals may range from adolescence to older adulthood. What differentiates domestic violence from other forms of family violence is that the relationship is supposedly equal, as opposed to a child and parent/adult relationship, or an adult child and his or her elderly parent.

Differing definitions between professionals of the various forms of violence become a problem when screening individuals for a program as well as when evaluating treatment outcome. Therefore it is important to specifically define those behaviors that constitute each form of violence. Physical and sexual violence are less difficult to define than psychological violence, as we shall discuss later in this chapter.

I have developed a Violence Inventory (commercially available through author) as part of a comprehensive lethality assessment questionnaire for domestic violence clients. The Violence Inventory, an extensive list of physical, sexual, and psychological acts of violence, can be completed by the interviewer with the client in order to assess the extent of previous acts of violence.

PHYSICAL VIOLENCE

Although physical violence may appear on the surface to be easily defined, many men enter into counseling with a limited definition of what constitutes physical violence. This may in part be attributed to patterns of minimization and denial, but it may also relate to society's perceptions of violence. We see so many severe acts of violence through the media that minor acts, such as pushing or grabbing, may not be consciously noticed at all. We have become desensitized to the most mild and frequently used acts of physical aggression.

For the purpose of treating male batterers, acts of physical violence include:

- Slapping
- Grabbing
- Punching
- Pushing
- Kicking
- Kneeing
- Choking
- Pushing to ground
- Biting
- Sitting or standing on
- Burning
- Spitting

- Drowning
- Hair-pulling
- Arm-twisting
- Hanging by neck, arms, or feet
- Handcuffing
- Tying up with rope
- Clawing or scratching
- Threatening with gun or knife
- Using knife or gun
- Threatening with object
- Using object
- Breaking or throwing objects

Using a consistent interview tool to assess the types, severity, and frequency of physical violence is important so that counselors do not overlook these details with any client. Denial, minimization, and simple lack of memory can prevent clients themselves from fully disclosing the extent of their violent behavior. Therefore it is up to the counselor to ask about specific acts, as described above, in order to make accurate determinations as to both potential lethality and a treatment plan that addresses the client's needs. Additionally, many clients do not consider pushing or grabbing "violence," so that an open-ended style of questioning alone is not likely to obtain descriptions of these less-than-lethal forms of physical violence. Additionally, asking direct questions about the specifics of their violence helps to break patterns of minimization and denial. The Violence Inventory inquires into the specific acts of violence, their frequency, and any injuries that have resulted from those acts.

Because of the difficulty in obtaining accurate information from abusers as to the extent, severity, and frequency of their violence, it is important for counselors to conduct separate interviews with the partners of their clients. There are several purposes for these interviews. The first is to obtain a more accurate violence history. Although victim's accounts of violence may also be prone to minimization or memory loss, experience has shown that they are likely to be more accurate than their abusing counterparts. Second, conducting a thorough violence history with the victim helps her to break any tendencies to minimize or deny the seriousness of her situation. Lastly, perpetrator-counseling programs are encouraged to maintain contact with the partner to determine if there are any additional acts of violence. This is especially important if the client is having contact with her. How these follow-up interviews are handled is discussed later in this book.

SEXUAL VIOLENCE

Because of both counselor and client's discomfort in discussing sexuality in general, sexual violence is often not addressed. However, research indicates that this form of violence may occur in over fifty percent of physically violent relationships. Many acts of sexual aggression also occur in concert with physical violence.

Acts of sexual violence include:

- Forced intercourse
- Beating on genitals
- Inserted objects
- Forced prostitution
- Forced masturbation
- Forced pornography
- Forced anal intercourse
- Forced sex with others
- Forced oral sex

In addition, many men use psychological violence (e.g., intimidation and coercion) in order to engage their partner in sexual activity. Counselors should take special care to discuss these matters with men on a regular basis once they have developed sufficient rapport.

PSYCHOLOGICAL VIOLENCE

Psychological violence has been defined in a number of ways over the years. Unlike physical and sexual violence, psychologically violent acts can range from the overt ("I'm going to kill you.") to the subtle ("If you leave, I can't be held responsible for what I do."). Only recently has there been any attempt to define it in any measurable way. It is important to arrive at clearly defined behaviors that constitute psychological violence, because it can be as emotionally damaging as physical or sexual assaults. However, many programs across the country use different definitions, which may add to confusion as to what counseling approach is best for your clients. Let's examine the various definitions of psychological violence used by programs today.

DULUTH MODEL

Certain programs, such as the Domestic Containment Program in Duluth, Minnesota (Pense and Paymar, 1993), have used the most inclusive definition of psychological violence. This is likely to define some men as batterers who in the past may have been labeled as abusive, unfair fighters, or chauvinistic. Their power and control wheel describes eight forms of psychological violence consisting of specific behaviors.

- **Using coercion and threats** (making and/or carrying out threats to do something to hurt her, threatening to leave her, to commit suicide, or to report her to welfare, making her drop charges, making her do illegal things)

- **Using economic power** (preventing her from getting or keeping a job, making her ask for money, giving her an allowance, taking her money, not letting her know about or have access to family income)

- **Using male privilege** (treating her like a servant, making all the big decisions, acting like the master of the castle, being the one to define men and women's roles)

- **Using children** (making her feel guilty about the children, using the children to relay messages, using visitation to harass her, threatening to take away the children)

- **Minimizing, denying, and blaming** (making light of the abuse and not taking her concerns about it seriously, saying the abuse didn't happen, shifting responsibility for abusive behavior, saying she caused it)

- **Using isolation** (controlling what she does, who she sees and talks to, what she reads and where she goes, limiting her outside involvement, using jealousy to justify actions)

- **Using emotional abuse** (putting her down, making her feel bad about herself, calling her names, making her think she's crazy, playing mind games, humiliating her, making her feel guilty)

- **Using intimidation** (making her afraid by using looks, actions, gestures, smashing things, destroying her property, abusing pets, displaying weapons)

AMNESTY INTERNATIONAL DEFINITION OF PSYCHOLOGICAL VIOLENCE

Lenore Walker (1994), author and clinical psychologist, has suggested using the definition provided by Amnesty International (the human rights watch group) of psychological violence or terrorism because it closely resembles the ways that male batterers control and intimidate their partners.

1. Isolation of victim

2. Induced debility-producing exhaustion

3. Monopolization of perceptions, including obsessiveness and possessiveness

4. Threats, such as death to self, victim, family or friends, or sham executions

5. Degradation, including humiliation, denial of victim's power, and verbal name-calling

6. Drug or alcohol administration

7. Altered states of consciousness produced by a hypnotic state

8. Occasional indulgences that keep hope alive that
the abuse will cease

Following are some examples of such actions as they might occur
in cases of domestic violence.

- Examples of **isolation** would include not letting her
socialize with friends or family members, forcing
her to stay at home or not letting her leave the
house without his presence, moving away from all
her support systems, such as friends or family
members.

- **Induced debility-producing exhaustion** would
include keeping her up all night during a fight,
waking her up to argue with her or abuse her
physically or sexually, making her do all the work at
home, forcing her into a servant role, keeping her
pregnant, or not allowing her to have support in
taking care of the children.

- **Monopolization of perceptions** includes pathological jealousy, having to know where she is all the
time and who she is with, accusing her of being
with other men, looking at other men, or wanting
to be with other men, following her, controlling
finances so she cannot leave him, stalking her after
a separation or divorce, or refusing to obey restraining orders. Stalking is a specific form of psychological violence to be described later in this chapter and
discussed more fully in Chapter Ten.

- **Threats** to kill her, kill others, or kill himself are
common forms of psychological abuse that are
intended to control her and get what he wants.

- **Verbal degradation** is another common behavior
that men use to cope with their fears, control their
partners, and deal with their own sense of worthlessness. Comparable to physical abuse, the verbal
name-calling has as much, or sometimes more,

impact on the victim in that it serves to damage the victim's sense of self-worth, resulting in feelings of powerlessness. She feels she must give up her own values, her point of view and feelings, in order to keep him from becoming physically violent.

- **Drug or alcohol administration** is common in many battering relationships. Many male batterers encourage their partner to use alcohol or drugs, some force her use of chemicals, and many battered women simply do so as a means of coping with their depression or anxiety about their situation. Women with preexisting chemical abuse problems often gravitate towards partners with similar problems. Frequently, violence is a prominent aspect of these relationships.

- **Altered states of consciousness** is a term that often refers to the batterer's attempt to invalidate his partner's perceptions. Many men try to convince their partner that she is crazy or is hearing or seeing things that did not happen, or that she can't live without him. The motion picture *Gaslight* quite effectively illustrates this dynamic.

- **The occasional indulgences** that we often hear are typified by the statement, "I promise dear, I'll never do it again." In psychological violence, this is followed with loving behavior, such as gift-giving, sensitivity, and tolerance for a short period of time before the old behavior sets in again.

This list provides a comprehensive description of psychological violence but is more narrow than the Duluth program definition. The Amnesty International definition describes the more severe forms of psychological violence without including what may be termed dysfunctional or negative interpersonal problem-solving behaviors. However, even many of these criteria are susceptible to interpretation and therefore may be criticized for not being clearly and consistently definable.

USING THE PENAL CODE TO DEFINE PSYCHOLOGICAL VIOLENCE

Use of the criminal penal code is one way of formulating a more clear and reliable definition of psychological violence. In most states a threat to hurt or batter is called *assault*. Simple assault may be a verbal act but is most commonly accompanied by a physical gesture, such as threatening with a fist or an object. Aggravated assault is usually a threat to kill as indicated by the use of a weapon, such as a knife or a gun. Threats to kill or terrorizing threats are also described in the penal code. Therefore, if we were to use the law as the criterion for defining psychological violence, then any threat to hurt or kill would be a part of this definition. Additionally, stalking would be an important part of this definition. Briefly, this includes any attempt on the perpetrator's behalf to follow, watch, harass, terrorize, or otherwise contact his partner against her desires.

The use of the penal code can be a good start in developing a working definition of psychological violence. Many of the men referred for treatment are court-ordered, and as a condition of probation or diversion are required to sign a statement indicating that they will abide by the court mandate as well as obey all laws. If the client threatens or assaults his partner, then he has broken the law and therefore is in violation of his probation or diversion. When this type of behavior is reported by the treatment program the criminal justice system is likely to respond, as opposed to the mere reporting of an argument where the man called his wife a derogatory name.

On the other hand, the obvious problem with using the penal code is its narrow and restrictive definition of psychological violence. Name-calling, for example, can over time be experienced as painful and traumatic as a physical threat of violence. Not addressing this fact in counseling gives the message that any behavior is acceptable as long as it is not illegal.

INVENTORY OF PSYCHOLOGICAL VIOLENCE TOWARDS WOMEN

Developed by Richard Tolman (1989) at the University of Illinois School of Social Work, the Psychological Violence towards Women Inventory is the first psychometric-type test that has been developed for specifically measuring psychological violence by male batterers. Tolman developed items that fell into six categories:

1. Attacking her personhood, demeaning, belittling, undermining self-worth

2. Defining her reality, getting her to question her own perceptions and judgments

3. Controlling her contact with outside world and support systems

4. Demanding subservience, complying with rigid sex-role expectations within the family

5. Withholding positive reinforcers within the relationship

6. Threatening nonphysical punishment for noncompliance with requests; status and emotional regulation

After analyzing the fifty-eight-statement questionnaire using responses of both battered women and male batterers, Tolman found that statements fell into one of two categories: domination/isolation (which included isolation from resources, demands for subservience, and rigid observance of traditional sex roles) and emotional/verbal (which included verbal attacks, behavior that demeans the woman, and withholding of emotional resources).

PSYCHOLOGICAL MALTREATMENT TOWARDS CHILDREN

Psychologists in the child maltreatment field have been working hard to understand the effects of psychological maltreatment so that a mandated reporter can better identify such situations.

Marla Brassard and Stuart Hart (Brassard, et al., 1993), from the University of Indiana, are two of the leading authorities in the field of psychological maltreatment of children. Through their efforts, a concise definition of psychological maltreatment of children is well on the way to being developed. The most recent definition is as follows:

- **Spurning:** rejecting (refusing to acknowledge or help, treating differently from others in ways that suggest dislike), degrading (depreciating, calling stupid or worthless, publicly humiliating)

- **Terrorizing:** intimidation, fear, violent dread, fright, witnessing extreme violence towards others, which includes witnessing the threat of serious injury or death, or the actual infliction of serious injury or death, threats to kill

- **Isolating:** separating from others, locking in a closet, room, not allowing to socialize with peers or other family members

- **Corrupting:** modeling pathological, violent, antisocial, or self-destructive behavior, alcohol and drug abuse, which includes the misuse/abuse of alcohol and drugs as administered or encouraged by the parent/caregiver

- **Exploiting:** using for one's own advantage or profit, forcing to take on the role of a servant, forcing or coercing to partake in pornography or prostitution

- **Denying emotional responsiveness:** the "depriva-
  tion suffered when a parent does not provide the
  normal experiences producing feelings of being
  loved, wanted, secure, and worthy." Emotional
  neglect is the failure to take into account or respond
  to the basic emotional needs of a child; the failure
  to treat them as human beings. Abandonment
  would also fall under this category.

This definition of psychological maltreatment is fairly consistent
with the other broader definitions described above. However, for our
purposes, some of the terminology would need to be changed to relate to a battered adult partner rather than a child.

WHICH DEFINITION TO USE?

Given these definitions of psychological violence, it is doubtful that
any of us have escaped being victims or perpetrators at one time or
another (e.g., wanting to make a unilateral decision on a particular
matter; being called by or calling our partner "stupid," or being publicly humiliated by a partner). However, most of us probably experienced or perpetrated these acts under conditions that lacked sufficient
intensity, frequency, and duration to have lasting negative effects.
This is probably not the case in many batterers' lives. It is the extreme, frequent, and consistent experience of psychological violence
that we need to look for and document if it exists. While each type of
psychological violence described above is distinct in principle, in practice there is a great deal of overlap, so that we rarely see only one type
of psychological violence. Therefore, no matter what definition or
combination of definitions you use, it is important for a client to
understand each type of psychological abuse he has perpetrated and
the effects of that abuse on his partner.

Researchers in the field of child maltreatment have been examining the issue of defining psychological abuse for many years. Like
family violence advocates, researchers, and clinicians, they have
struggled with the advantages and disadvantages of broad versus

narrow definitions of psychological maltreatment. Broad definitions of psychological abuse recognize its manifestations in both obvious and subtle forms. Broad definitions also help to clearly illustrate the pervasiveness of this type of abuse and the gray boundary between abusive and nonabusive behaviors. Broad definitions make the connection between social and cultural factors and their influence on the experience of the individual or family. On the other hand, these broad definitions of psychological abuse may often disregard important individual and cultural differences creating standards of conduct defined by a few but compared to many. The greatest drawback to broad definitions of psychological abuse is that the definition may be so vague or general that it makes the majority of parents (or men) vulnerable to being identified as abusers. This also gives the subtle or direct impression that these "borderline" cases will eventually become full-fledged cases of physical or sexual abuse, even though there is no definitive research that supports this theory.

Narrow definitions tend to restrict the list of actions constituting psychological maltreatment to the more blatant and more easily agreed-upon behaviors that constitute psychological abuse. By their less-inclusive nature, these definitions are less vulnerable to the problems of the broader definitions. However, these more-narrow definitions often ignore the subtle forms of abuse that may be equally injurious as, or predictive of, the more serious forms. Narrow definitions may also fail to identify social forms of psychological abuse such as racism and sexism.

Another issue related to definition of psychological maltreatment is how one determines what acts constitute psychological abuse. Is it the act *per se* that is abusive, or is it the effect it has on the victim? Simply defining acts as abusive does not take into account the range of possible reactions by individuals. There is still much research that is needed as to what acts have what effects under what circumstances (severity, frequency, etc.). Another question needing exploration is the effect of repeated abuse over time. Is there an accumulation of psychological effects over time, making a person more vulnerable to psychological injury and less able to defend against psychological attacks on the self?

With child victims, the stage of development plays an important role in what constitutes psychological maltreatment and its subsequent effects. Particular acts of abuse may have a more devastating effect on a younger child than an adolescent. Considerable research has supported that early psychological maltreatment may have profound and lasting effects on children, leading them to experience many of the same problems as those who have been physically and sexually abused. Developmental issues play less of a significant role with adult victims of psychological abuse. However, adults who are victims of repeated trauma may experience a diminishing of internal psychological defenses and resources necessary to fend off the negative effects of abuse over time.

Another problem in accurately defining psychological maltreatment has to do with the issue of intent. It has been suggested that a victim's past experiences may either exacerbate or diminish the effects of the abuse. For example, a person whose self-esteem has been damaged by past acts of violence may define some acts as more abusive than an objective outsider would. Even some individuals who have greater psychological resources may experience a particular negative comment or abusive action in a detrimental manner.

It is clear from the literature that there are more questions than answers regarding definitions of psychological maltreatment. Therefore, counselors are encouraged to cautiously use a definition of psychological maltreatment, particularly when working with court-mandated clients and handling crises. Because psychological abuse is likely to regularly occur with male batterers in treatment, it is suggested that counselors clarify with probation, the courts, and clients themselves what acts of psychological abuse will be considered a reoffense and therefore reported to the court (or probation). Similarly, it is suggested that counselors use caution when using psychological abuse as a basis of exercising their duty to protect when that would necessitate a violation of confidentiality and/or call for involuntary hospitalization. In these situations, I would recommend that counselors use the more narrow, crime-specific definitions of psychological violence (threats, harassing, stalking, etc.) and reserve the broader elements of the definition (name-calling, using male privilege, etc.) for the education component of the treatment program.

REFERENCES

Brassard, M.R.; Hart, S.N.; and Hardy, D.B. (1993). The psychological maltreatment rating scales. *Child Abuse and Neglect,* v17 (6), 715-730.

Pense, Ellen and Paymar, Michael (1993). *Education groups for men who batter: The Duluth Model.* New York: Springer Publications.

Tolman, R.M. (1989). The development of a measure of psychological maltreatment of women by their male partners. *Violence and Victims,* Fall, v4 (3), 159-178.

Walker, L.E.A. (1994). *Abused women and survivor therapy: A practical guide for the psychotherapist.* Washington, DC: APA Press.

CHAPTER THREE

What Counseling Approach Should I Use?

The first step to developing a program or simply offering counseling services to male batterers is to establish a theoretical model from which to structure your interventions. You must ask yourself: why does a man abuse his partner? Interventions will be structured depending on the answer to this question. As indicated in the introductory chapter, we are far from knowing the definitive answer to this question. Therefore, it is up to you, the reader, to become familiar with the literature to date and make a decision as to which path to take. Remember, the specific character of theory may not be as important to stopping violence as the fact that it is *an intervention.*

The most common approaches used in counseling male batterers are those that emphasize:

1. Cognitive-behavioral interventions,

2. Sex-role issues, power, control, and violence against women (educational-profeminist interventions),

3. A family systems orientation, or

4. An individual psychodynamic orientation.

31

I felt that it would be helpful for the reader to reduce the approaches to counseling male batterers into four broad categories; however, in reality the programs across the country are hybrids, in that they utilize any number of these and other approaches as a basis for their treatment interventions. For example, some programs combine the cognitive interventions with education on gender analysis and incorporate couples or individual treatment in an adjunctive manner. Let's briefly examine these approaches more closely and then discuss their relative strengths and weaknesses.

COGNITIVE-BEHAVIORAL APPROACHES

Since the late 1970s when Anne Ganley and Lance Harris developed their inpatient counseling program at American Lakes Veterans Hospital in Tacoma, Washington, their innovations have set a standard for working with male batterers (Ganley and Harris, 1978; Ganley, 1981, 1987). They wrote about using anger-management techniques, such as the time-out, to help men learn to recognize and control their emotions to prevent outbursts of aggressive behavior. They focused exclusively on the man, with the rationale being that he was the violent one and therefore needed to learn how to control his behavior. In addition to the anger-management skills, clients also explored issues relating to sex-role socialization, communication, and the use of alcohol and drugs.

The basis for their interventions was social learning theory. In a nutshell, social learning theory posits that we learn behaviors as children through observations of others and through our own direct experience. Ganley and Harris discovered that many of the men who battered their partners also grew up in homes where they either were abused or witnessed their father abuse their mother. These authors believed that male batterers learned through observation as children that violence is an acceptable way of dealing with anger and conflict. Therefore, as adults they would use violence to cope with their anger and conflict in their interpersonal relationships. Social learning theory also suggests that we learn from direct experience. When men become angry and subsequently violent, there is a build-up of bodily tension that disappears afterwards. In this way the relief from tension becomes a reinforcer for their violence. When social systems, such as the police and courts, fail to appropriately respond to domestic violence, this too could reinforce the behavior of the batterer. Ganley and Harris therefore supported the notion of court-mandated counseling so that men get the message from the community (police and the courts) that violence is not acceptable.

Counselors utilizing a cognitive-behavioral approach to treating male batterers use a wide variety of techniques and interventions. Heavy emphasis is placed on the use of the time-out and other anger-management techniques to help men learn more adaptive ways of coping with conflict. However, many counselors (Saunders, 1989) also apply cognitive therapy techniques in helping batterers change the dysfunctional thought patterns that lead to emotional arousal and perhaps violence.

According to cognitive therapy theory (Beck, 1976; Persons, 1989), what a person feels is influenced (but not totally controlled) by their thoughts. Ultimately both thoughts and feelings determine a person's actions. By changing thought patterns through cognitive therapy, a person is likely to "feel" better. Constructive, realistic attitudes in combination with positive emotions are likely to result in healthier functioning.

In treatment of male batterers, cognitive interventions are specifically directed towards dysfunctional thinking processes that serve to escalate anxiety and anger, and increase the possibility for violence. Interventions are geared toward teaching men how to soothe their own feelings that result from their dysfunctional thinking, rather than looking to external factors (such as controlling their partner through violence) to achieve this goal.

One of the primary methods through which these programs help clients control their maladaptive thought process is the use of journals to record thoughts, feelings, or anger. Clients learn to identify and write down their negative self-talk, so they can eventually recognize the dysfunctional thinking before it can escalate their emotions and make them vulnerable to acting violent. Other techniques for

control of dysfunctional thoughts include self-soothing talk, medita-
tion, and relaxation. Many of these cogitive therapy programs also
incorporate a great deal of education on the dynamics of domestic
violence.

FEMINIST-ORIENTED APPROACHES

At the same time that Ganley and Harris were developing their inpatient program in Seattle, another program was being developed by
a group three thousand miles away in Boston named EMERGE
(Adams, 1986). Growing out of the men's consciousness-raising
movement, EMERGE was a feminist-based program that approached
the problem of battering from a sociopolitical perspective, rather than
a psychological perspective. The focus in their groups was on exploi-
tation of women through men's use of techniques (physical, sexual,
and psychological violence) that upset the balance of power between
men and women. They saw the main purpose for men's violence
against women to be an effort to maintain control and power rather
than a result of psychological deficiencies. Although they used many
of the techniques described as cognitive-behavioral approaches to
treatment, the primary focus of their education groups (not therapy)
was the gender analysis of the problem.

EMERGE and other profeminist programs, such as the Domestic Containment Program in Duluth, Minnesota (Paymar, 1993), tend
to call their interventions *education* and not *therapy*. Historically these
groups have usually been run by either former batterers or men interested in the issue from a political perspective rather than by licensed
mental health providers. In recent years, however, this trend has
changed somewhat; there are more mental health providers who are
now interested in this issue, not only from a professional viewpoint
but from a political perspective as well. This is a positive sign that a
sociopolitical analysis of this problem is beginning to be incorporated into traditional mental health training programs.

The crucial difference between the profeminist approach to treating male batterers and other psychological approaches is that the

profeminist approach focuses on the sexist attitudes that are precipitants of violence rather than the psychological causes. Additionally, profeminist programs tend to minimize the differences between batterers and nonbatterers, allowing the men to look at the ways in which all men devalue women and assert their male privilege. Heavy emphasis is placed on the man examining how his behavior has affected his partner or family, and ways that he can make them safe from his violence.

Group sessions include education on the causes of violence, sexism, etc., as well as the effects of the man's violence on his partner and his children. Because the program focuses on the outcome of violence rather than psychopathology, heavy emphasis is placed on power and control (as described in the Duluth model of psychological violence) and therefore on all the ways that men dominate and control their partners (e.g., using coercion and threats; using economic power; using male privilege; using children; minimizing, denying, and blaming; using isolation; using emotional abuse; using intimidation). The group sessions are highly structured (as with the cognitive-behavioral approach) with clearly articulated goals and expectations of the participants.

COUPLES/FAMILY SYSTEMS APPROACHES

After the late 1970s a number of programs across the country were utilizing an approach to treatment focused on the couple relationship or the family rather than the individual. Programs such as those of the Mental Research Institute in Palo Alto, California (Everstine and Everstine, 1993) and Robert Geffner and Carol Mantooth (Mantooth, et al., 1987) in Tyler, Texas, were addressing the marital dynamics of family violence. From proponents of the profeminist and cognitive-behavioral approaches, they received heavy criticism then, and still are today, for "blaming the victim" by implying that she must be a part of the problem if her participation in treatment is necessary to stop the violence. However, those who choose this method of addressing the problem state that the issue of blame is not relevant, that both partners participate in maladaptive ways of interacting with one another, and that the focus of counseling is to change these patterns. One outgrowth of these programs would be the cessation of violence, and the ultimate goal was to help couples achieve a more rewarding relationship. They saw, and perhaps rightfully so, that focusing only on the batterer does nothing to change the unhealthy marital dynamics that in part gave rise to the violence. Many of the couples/family therapy proponents also point to the fact that the research (the famous study by Straus, Gelles, and Steinmetz described earlier) indicates that both husbands and wives participate in violence (although the women usually receive greater injuries) and therefore interventions should be directed towards both.

Like the profeminist and cognitive-behavioral approaches, couples/families approaches vary from individual/program to individual/program. Because there are many different approaches to couples and family therapy, it would be impossible to describe in detail how each one would address the issue of violence. Instead I would like to generally describe how a couples/family therapist may approach the issue of family violence.

Let me begin by saying that it is possible to conduct successful couples or family therapy without giving the partner the message that she is the reason for his violence. In fact, most couples therapists with whom I have spoken have indicated that this "blaming" is actually one of the problems these couples already engage in. An unwary therapist might only be reinforcing this maladaptive pattern rather than changing it. So it would be important to begin any couples treatment by telling each person that they and only they are responsible for their own behavior, whether we are talking about physical or psychological violence, reliability in keeping agreements, their communication patterns, or any other behavior.

The systems therapist views the individual as a part, not the whole. The individual is part of a family, a community, a city and country, and so on. Therefore, individuals do not act solely alone but in response to others around them. This basic philosophy is what differentiates systems-oriented therapists from others. Systems theory plays down the significance of how individual psychopathology causes certain problems, and rather focuses on how individuals behave and respond to their social contexts.

In treating any family or couple, the systems therapist's goal is to make what are called second-order changes. A first-order change is a change in behavior — for example, the man taking time-outs when he is angry or the woman not stopping the man from taking a time-out during an argument. There can be changes in behavior without essential changes in the relationship dynamic. In other words, there may still exist a dynamic where the man and woman do not experience equality by either sharing control or at least taking turns being in control. Instead, the individuals may have changed specific behaviors, such as by taking a time-out, while the dynamic of victim and victimizer still remains. For a second-order change to occur, both members of the couple must experience a change in how they view power and control, communication, and the meaning of intimacy. This goal, of course, is easy to discuss in theory; to achieve it in reality is another matter.

Couples programs vary from counselor to counselor; however, many employ techniques similar to those of cognitive-behavioral and profeminist programs. Time-outs, communication skills, role playing, and education about family violence are often an integral part of the couples/family sessions. Counselors often find that blaming the perpetrator or the victim is neither constructive nor serves as a positive role model for either the man or the woman. Instead, counselors find it important to take a nonblaming, neutral stance. Couples therapists may "reframe" the situation from being a violence problem to a need for being heard or creating distance during an argument. It is understood that this need does not justify the violence — but also that there may be yet another intent, which the man is unable to realize because of lack of perceived options. The growth model notion of "positive intent" suggests that individuals sometimes act in ways that suggest a need that is not being met in some other more adaptive manner. In other words, the individual's maladaptive behaviors may have a positive intent but ultimately cause others to respond in equally maladaptive ways that may only further serve to escalate the interactive patterns.

Initially the couples therapist is likely to focus on the beginning of the most recent argument: how it escalated, what each person was wanting from the other, and lastly, how they could have communicated differently. One assumption in the counseling is that the better the communication patterns, the less likely the argument will escalate to the point that either one is acting irrationally. The systems therapist will not just focus on the arguments, however, but also examine the fundamental dynamics that give rise to all maladaptive patterns in their relationship. The goal is to facilitate the couple in changing the ways they view themselves and each other so that they experience a healthier interpersonal relationship.

PSYCHODYNAMIC APPROACHES

One does not read much in the literature about doing long-term psychodynamically-oriented psychotherapy with male batterers. I believe this is related to several reasons. First, the majority of batterers are not amenable to long-term, insight-oriented psychotherapy. This is because many men see therapy in general as being for crazy or weak individuals. Men also view therapy as needing help, which many do not like to admit to themselves, let alone someone else. Traditional psychodynamically oriented therapy involves exploring inner thoughts, fantasies, feelings, etc., a process that men are not typically inclined to do on a regular basis. The slow process of change that results from this type of therapy may be experienced as frustrating to men who are more results/action-oriented. Today, this pattern is changing, and more and more men are entering into therapy to develop greater insight into themselves and those around them. But typically, the batterer who is not willing to examine his obvious destructive behaviors is not initially going to be interested in exploring a deeper psychological understanding of himself. Additionally, for many men, the cost of long-term, psychodynamically oriented psychotherapy may be prohibitive — particularly when there is no evidence that this approach to treatment is any more effective than shorter-term group interventions.

Another reason why we have not seen much literature on the individual treatment of male batterers is because the early writers on this issue (myself included) initially downplayed the utility of traditional insight-oriented psychotherapy. Doing so ultimately limited the discussion of the treatment issue to the other three approaches described above. Perhaps it was thought that the most traditional psychodynamic approaches, because of their less directive structure, did not directly address the violence and may have either given tacit approval for the behavior or implied blame toward the victim. In either case, this has been unfortunate. After many years of working with male batterers, I have discovered that some men may be quite amenable to and benefit from long-term, psychodynamically oriented therapy as opposed to shorter-term, cognitive-behavioral approaches to treatment.

It is quite possible to use an insight-oriented approach with male batterers while simultaneously addressing the issues of domestic violence. Depending on one's clinical orientation, the counselor may begin to explore the needs, thoughts, and feelings that the client may have been experiencing at the time of his violent acting-out so that the man begins to develop a greater awareness of the affective, cognitive, and behavioral precursors to the crisis. Behavioral interventions, such as the time-out, may be utilized in conjunction with this approach to help the client employ other strategies to solving conflict and disagreement.

As a Jungian-oriented therapist, I have found it quite helpful for men to explore their inner world through the use of dreams and active imagination. For some men, the discovery that they possess undeveloped or unaware aspects of their personality, such as the feminine aspects of the psyche, can be both shocking and frightening as well as intriguing and exciting. In addition, many male batterers have had negative experiences with their primary care-givers that have left strong, and often unconscious, emotional complexes. These are likely to get reenacted in their intimate relationships. Developing an awareness of these powerful, and yet unconscious, emotions can be an important first step in taking control of the violence. The simple awareness or consciousness of these emotions can diminish their power. Subsequently, as the man becomes more comfortable with recognizing and understanding the power that these unconscious forces have had on his life, he can begin to exercise greater control of their expression before they develop in intensity. As with a natural disaster, we can do a lot to minimize the damage if we can predict its occurrence.

Insight-oriented counseling also offers the client a much greater opportunity to explore issues of childhood abuse. Through his therapy, the client can explore the long-term effects of child maltreatment on his attitudes, feelings, and behaviors. Doing so allows the man to develop greater awareness of what psychological issues, beliefs, expectations, etc., he brings to his interactions with his partner and how they ultimately manifest in relationship problems. For many men, resolving childhood traumas will be the center of focus during the initial stages of therapy (Sonkin, 1992). Therapists are encouraged to receive additional training in this specialized area of psychology.

The relationship between the therapist and the client plays an important part in psychodynamically oriented therapy. Because of the intimate nature of the relationship and the perceived power/authority differential, the psychotherapist-client interaction can provide fertile ground for the client to act out his unconscious psychological material in therapy. This must occur in a safe place, so that the client has the opportunity to become conscious of the acting-out and subsequently begin to develop a new relationship to his own inner world and ultimately with others.

Obviously, this brief discussion of psychodynamic psychotherapy only begins to scratch the surface as to how it may be helpful in treating male batterers. As I have already mentioned, there are many men who could benefit from such an approach by a skilled therapist knowledgeable in the dynamics of domestic violence. Additionally, there are also many men who are participating in a structured domestic violence program who may need the additional attention that an individual therapist could provide. Male batterers suffer from a variety of psychological problems that ultimately manifest in their violent behaviors. For some of these individuals, those problems may be best addressed in a more traditional psychotherapeutic setting as long as they are amenable to such a treatment approach.

STRENGTHS AND WEAKNESSES

With any individual or social problem, the most outspoken individuals or groups usually have strongest opinions about why it is occurring in the first place and how to best address a particular situation. So it is for the issue of domestic violence. Proponents of the four approaches described above have all made strong arguments justifying their approach to treating male batterers. However, as I stated earlier, this is all within the context of no research that indicates that one approach is necessarily better than another. In fact, it is not clear if it is a particular kind of intervention (cognitive-behavioral, profeminist, individual, couples) that is effective, or the simple fact of an intervention (as opposed to doing nothing) that is the significant variable in this discussion. Until we have more definitive answers, we are left with a number of good theories that on the surface make sense and that, for some individuals, have been shown to be effective to varying degrees in stopping domestic violence.

Most theories have their strengths and, of course, their limitations, and these four approaches are not an exception to that rule. Because domestic violence is so pervasive, affecting families of all ethnic, socioeconomic, and religious backgrounds, no one approach is going to be effective with all persons experiencing this problem. This statement is also true for other problems whether they are medical, psychological, or social in nature. Complex dilemmas demand complex solutions, and varying approaches are therefore needed to address different aspects of the problem.

Each of these theoretical approaches to counseling male batterers can, in its own way, be right — not unlike the story of three blind persons and the elephant. Each grasps a part of the animal and is convinced that it is shaped like a trunk, leg, or tail when in fact they are only seeing (or feeling) part of the whole picture. Each approach is valid in that it addresses an important part of the whole animal. The cognitive-behavioral counselor is paying close attention to how the escalation process develops as a result of dysfunctional thought patterns and poor or undeveloped skills at coping with emotional turmoil. The profeminist approach steps back and looks at the social-political determinants of the issue of violence against women — this problem does not occur within a vacuum of a single relationship or family. Understanding the social pressure for men to act in ways that support or certainly lay the foundation for violence is a critical point that must not be forgotten by either counselors or clients. The psychodynamic-oriented counselor is able to help the client become more aware of his interpersonal relationships as well as understand the long-term effects of childhood abuse and how to change maladaptive patterns of relating to self and others. Lastly, the couples and family therapists have made a valuable contribution to this field by depathologizing the individual and focusing on the interaction between family members, which not only can serve to de-escalate conflict but enhance marital/family satisfaction altogether.

Counselors using a cognitive-behavioral or a systems approach, by focusing on the individual or couples dynamics, may fail to address issues relating to power, control, and gender. If issues relating to power and control are not addressed, the clients fail to understand how violence ultimately affects the partner and serves to maintain an atmosphere of fear and distrust in the family. However, the profeminist approach may not pay enough attention to the escalation process either from the individual or couple perspective, making change an intellectual and abstract process rather than relating to specific cognitive, emotional, or communication routines.

Another limitation of the cognitive-behavioral approach may be its tendency to pathologize the batterer, whereas both the profeminist and family systems approaches tend to place the counselor and client more on an equal level. The profeminist counselor talks about how all men struggle with issues relating to power and control over women. The family systems therapist usually views the problem as being not within the individual but with the family/couple, thereby defusing the blame issue.

Couples and profeminist counselors, in their effort to keep the focus on the relationship and society, may fail to adequately predict dangerous behaviors — either homicide or suicide. This is particularly true for the profeminist counselor who has not received training as a mental health professional. Similarly, such a counselor may also fail to recognize when a batterer is suffering from a psychiatric disorder and in need of professional treatment. This may happen to a lesser extent with couples therapists, but nevertheless the same problem can occur with systems-oriented counselors who view all problems as stemming from dysfunctional family interactions.

Each of these approaches addresses three important aspects of domestic violence treatment: arousal control, gender issues, and marital dynamics. It is unclear whether one or another, or a combination of all three, is necessary to stop violent behavior. I have visited programs across the country and abroad, and many report a high success rate. This fact suggests to me that perhaps the most important variable in the successful treatment of male batterers is a thoughtful treatment or education plan that provides tools and education within the context of a community ethic that does not tolerate violence in the family.

ECLECTIC APPROACHES

In light of the previous discussion of treatment approaches to domestic violence, it is clear that no one person can provide the definitive method of treating male batterers. Then how does one decide what approach to utilize with clients? A lot will depend on what method and philosophy you are most comfortable applying. Some counselors are more comfortable working with couples than individuals, or vice versa. Similarly, many counselors find semistructured, educationally oriented support groups easier to lead than the highly structured cognitive-behavioral therapy group or individual sessions. Some counselors may opt for a less structured men's support group or individual psychotherapy. Most importantly, counselors must be aware of what they can and cannot offer men experiencing domestic violence. If you have well-thought-out interventions that you believe will help to stop violent behavior, then apply those interventions and evaluate their effectiveness. Over the years, I have worked with a number of counselors who are more interested in providing adjunctive individual or group counseling for male batterers already participating in a batterer's treatment program than they are in providing the primary interventions geared toward stopping violence.

Many of the programs I have visited employ techniques from a variety of philosophies resulting in their own eclectic approach to counseling male batterers (Sonkin, Martin, and Walker, 1985). For example, the groups I have co-led in the past focused on anger management as well as gender issues. As an adjunct to the group experience, men participated in couples counseling so that the material being taught in the group was being applied at home with their partners. Although I have been described as using the cognitive-behavioral approach, I cannot say that I have strictly adhered to many of the principles of cognitive therapy (e.g., becoming aware of dysfunctional thought patterns). Instead I have put greater emphasis on the behavioral interventions relating to anger management as well as discussions of sex-role socialization and its effect on interpersonal relationships.

Most important in choosing a counseling approach is to understand that addressing the violent behavior must be a priority. Whether this is done in an educational or anger-management group, couples counseling, a profeminist program, or individual psychotherapy may not be as significant a variable as the consistency of the treatment rationale. Therefore, counselors should set up a mechanism for evaluating the effectiveness of their approach so as to adjust their interventions as needed throughout the treatment process.

REFERENCES

Adams, D.C. (1986). *Counseling men who batter: A profeminist analysis of clinical models.* Paper presented at the Annual Meeting of the American Psychiatric Association, May 14, 1986.

Beck, Aaron T. (1976). *Cognitive therapy and the emotional disorders.* New York: International Universities Press.

Everstine, D.S. and Everstine, L. (1993). *The trauma response: Treatment for emotional injury.* New York: W.W. Norton & Co., Inc.

Ganley, A. (1981). *Court-mandated counseling for men who batter* (participants and trainers manuals). Washington, DC: The Center for Women's Policy Studies.

Ganley, A. (1987). Perpetrators of domestic violence: An overview of counseling the court-mandated client. In: D.J. Sonkin (ed.), *Domestic violence on trial: Psychological and legal dimensions of family violence.* New York: Springer Publications.

Ganley, A. and Harris, L. (1978). *Domestic violence: Issues in designing and implementing programs for male batterers.* Paper presented at the 86th Annual Convention of the American Psychological Association, Toronto, Canada.

Mantooth, C.M.; Geffner, R.; Franks, D.; and Patrick, J. (1987). *Family violence: A treatment manual for reducing couple violence.* Tyler, TX: University of Texas at Tyler Press.

Paymar, Michael (1993). *Violent no more: Helping men end domestic abuse.* Alameda, CA: Hunter House.

Persons, Jacqueline (1989). *Cognitive therapy in practice: A case formulation approach.* New York: W.W. Norton & Co., Inc.

Saunders, D.G. (1989). Cognitive and behavioral interventions with men who batter: Applications and outcomes. In: P.L. Caesar and L.K. Hamberger (eds.), *Treating men who batter: Theory, practice and programs.* New York: Springer Publications.

Sonkin, D.J. (1992). *Wounded men: A man's guide to recovering from child abuse.* Stamford, CT: Long Meadow Press.

Sonkin, D.J.; Martin, D.; and Walker, L.E.A. (1985). *The male batterer: A treatment approach.* New York: Springer Publications.

CHAPTER FOUR

The Assessment Process

The assessment process for male batterers is in many ways not unlike the way one would assess any other client seen in a clinical practice or social service agency. However, because of the potential lethality inherent in domestic violence cases and the fact that many men are being ordered into counseling (by court or partner), and therefore often demonstrate low motivation for counseling, special procedures must be employed to set the stage for successful intervention outcome. Suggestions in this chapter are based on the Learning to Live without Violence Program.

INFORMED CONSENT

Setting session rules is an important part of the treatment process, for it creates the frame for the treatment program. It is crucial that each client agree to these rules and follow them exactly as they are set forth, to assure that they derive the most benefit from the experience. The informed consent should at a minimum include the confidentiality policy, how reoffenses will be handled, attendance requirement, alcohol and drug use before session, missed sessions, emergencies, fees, and termination. Below is an example of an informed consent form.

Welcome to Learning to Live without Violence. The primary goal of this program is to help you learn to prevent physical, sexual, and psychological violence in your interpersonal relationships. In order to help you best reach this goal, we have found it necessary for participants to agree to the following guidelines.

Confidentiality: By law and professional ethics, your sessions are strictly confidential. Generally, no information will be shared with anyone without your written permission. If you are seeing another therapist or health professional, it may be necessary for us to contact that person so that we can coordinate our efforts. If this is necessary we will ask for your permission. There are, however, a number of exceptions to this confidentiality policy.

1. If we are ordered by the court to testify or release records.

2. If you are a victim or perpetrator of child abuse, we are required by law to report this to the authorities responsible for investigating child abuse.

3. If you are a victim or perpetrator of elder abuse, we are required by law to report this to Adult Protective Services or other appropriate authorities.

4. If you threaten harm to yourself or someone else, we may be required to call the police and warn the potential victim, or take other reasonable steps to prevent the harm.

If you are mandated by the court to attend these sessions, we will need to have your permission to speak with the probation department or other criminal justice agency that is monitoring your compliance with the court orders. In these conversations we will be reporting the following information:

1. Reoffenses of violence towards anyone

2. Violations of court orders

3. Missed appointments

4. Participation in session (verbal participation and completion of homework)

5. Compliance with session rules

It is also important that clients respect the confidentiality of your fellow session members. Therefore, it is very important that participants not disclose any information discussed by other group members to anyone outside of the session, including counselors, probation officers, partners, friends, and family members.

Partner contact. It is a requirement of your participation in Learning to Live without Violence that counselors meet with your partner before you are accepted into the program. Once you are accepted into the program, we will have weekly phone contact with your partner to assess whether or not you have perpetrated violence and to receive feedback on how you are incorporating the educational material from your counseling sessions into your relationship. In addition, every six weeks we will meet with you and your partner to evaluate your progress in counseling and determine if additional treatment options are necessary. If you are separated or divorced from your partner, we must have contact with any subsequent individuals with whom you become emotionally involved. This can be very difficult for some men because it involves their telling their new partner about their history of violence. If you are truly committed to changing your pattern of coping with conflict and emotional stress, we strongly encourage you to inform any new romantic attachments of your history of violence and participation in this program. **These partner follow-up policies are a requirement for all participants in our program.**

Alcohol and other drugs. No alcohol or other drugs are to be used twenty-four hours before you attend each session. All clients are encouraged to abstain altogether while you are in the program. Some clients will be required to attend additional alcohol or drug treatment as a requirement for participation in the program.

Attendance. Members are required to attend the entire session (fifty minutes for individual sessions, one hundred and twenty minutes for group sessions). Once the group sessions begin, there will be no admittance and therefore latecomers will be considered absent. Give yourself plenty of travel time so that you arrive before the session begins. **You are only allowed to miss one group session for every twelve-week cycle.**

No violence in the session. This rule speaks for itself. This includes psychological violence as well. If you break this rule, it will result in automatic dismissal from the program. No weapons are to be brought into the building (including firearms, pocket knives, mace, etc.). If you break this rule, it will result in automatic dismissal from the program.

Emergencies: We are available in the evenings and on the weekends for emergencies. Leave a message on our voice mail and we will call you back as soon as we retrieve the message. If you need immediate assistance, call the office first for emergency instructions and leave a message. If you need to page us, use a touch-tone phone and dial (555) 555-5555; after the brief message, punch in your phone number and we will call you back as soon as possible. **There is no charge for brief phone calls.** There will be a charge for extended calls (more than fifteen minutes), repeated phone sessions, or emergency sessions in person at the office or hospital.

Contact with other clients. At the beginning of a session cycle, we will encourage members to exchange telephone numbers. Each new member will be assigned a "buddy" who will help orient him to the session process and be available during times of crisis.

Terminating treatment: You have the right to terminate or take a break from your treatment at any time without our permission or agreement. However, if you do decide to exercise this option, and you are on diversion or probation, your probation officer will be notified immediately. We encourage you to talk with us about the reason for your decision in a counseling session so that we can bring sufficient closure to our work together. In our final session we can discuss your progress thus far and explore ways in which you can continue to utilize the skills and knowledge that you have gained through your counseling. We will also discuss our concerns and recommend ways to address them. Referrals will be given should you desire them.

Licensed mental health professionals are ethically required to continue therapeutic relationships only so long as it is reasonably clear that patients are benefiting from the relationship. Therefore, if we believe that you need additional treatment, or if we believe that we can no longer help you with your problems, we will discuss this with you and make an appropriate referral.

Please sign this form and keep a copy for yourself for future reference. Should you have any questions at any time, please ask.

I have read, understand and agree to the information and policies described in this patient information form.

Name _____ Date _____

INITIAL ASSESSMENT

The goal of the first interview is to set the ground rules for counseling, develop rapport, assess the motivation and suitability for the program, provide the client with initial tools to begin to take responsibility for his actions, and prevent further violence. Potential candidates must be evaluated prior to being accepted into the program to see if they will be able to make use of your particular treatment interventions. During this period of data gathering, the counselor is evaluating the client's motivation for change. It is expected that the man may agree to the program simply because it is better than going to jail and not because there is a genuine desire to change. He is not likely to feel that he *wants* to change, but that he *has* to because of external factors. Some men may come into an evaluation session hostile and oppositional in attitude. Such behavior should not by itself be sufficient to reject a candidate although, if accompanied by other factors including a high degree of lethality, it may indicate that he is not ready for the program.

The two most important criteria for selection are the assessment of lethality and desire to change. The majority of men will acknowledge that their violence is a problem in need of changing. Those men who adamantly state that they have a right to be violent and have no desire to change generally are not good candidates for a treatment program outside of a locked facility. An individual with this attitude should, as a rule, be considered at high risk for reoffending.

High-lethality cases, as a rule, should not be considered for a standard outpatient treatment program without other measures being taken to assure the safety of the potential victim(s) (i.e., electronic monitoring, work furlough programs, etc.). Many male batterers require a period of incarceration or hospitalization in order to restabilize them for an outpatient treatment program. The Learning to Live without Violence Program is designed for those batterers whose behavior needs immediate changing but are not so dangerous as to put others at the risk of being hurt. These men must be motivated enough to attend weekly sessions and utilize the educational material presented.

LETHALITY ASSESSMENT

Prediction of violence is a controversial concept in the field of psychology. Although some theoreticians say that violence prediction or lethality is an immeasurable concept in clinical practice and that professionals should refrain from making such predictions, others suggest that abandoning the attempt to make accurate predictions is somewhat premature at this time. Research has indicated that we are likely to be wrong as often as we are right about predicting violent behavior in the general clinical and criminal population. However, studies looking at factors that predict violence have shown that the best predictor of future behavior is past behavior. Therefore, a person who has established patterns of physical, sexual, or psychological violence towards his spouse is likely to continue that pattern unless he receives psychological treatment (and even then, the violence can reoccur). Domestic violence offenders are very predictable for this reason.

However, how does one differentiate the degrees of lethality within this particular population? Mostly from common sense, and secondly from a thorough lethality assessment. In general, all forms of violence are potentially lethal. One could die from a push that results in a fall down a flight of stairs or by hitting one's head on certain types of furniture as easily as one could die from being strangled. However, some forms of violence are inherently more lethal, even though lesser forms of violence can also cause serious injury or death. Therefore, in order to differentiate candidates for your program you need to make the judgment that a slap, although illegal, in general is less lethal than choking to the point of unconsciousness.

LETHALITY RESEARCH

A study by Dr. Angela Browne (1987) of forty-two family homicides, in which battered women killed or seriously injured their abusive partners, showed an apparent correspondence between lethality and certain characteristics of adult relationships controlled by violent men. In comparing the relationships of women who later killed their abusers with assault-only cases (in which women were battered but did not kill or seriously injure their abusive mates), the researcher found that what discriminated between the two groups were the following variables:

1. Man's frequency of violence

2. Man's severity of violence

3. Man's frequency of intoxication

4. Man's drug use

5. Man's threats to kill

6. Man's forced/threatened sexual acts

7. Women's suicide threats

Although this study does not give definitive answers as to the ability to predict time and place with regard to lethality, it does shed light on the ability to predict who may be at risk for committing or becoming the victim of lethal violence. What is interesting to note about this study is that all but one of these variables were based on the abusive man's behavior. When the women in this study realized that the violence was only going to escalate and not stop, they attacked the batterer in defense of their own lives.

ASSESSING DANGER

In assessing for lethality, it is important to take into account the above-mentioned factors as an integral part of the evaluation process. In order to get a thorough description of the types and frequency of violence perpetrated by the client, the Violence Inventory-Lethality Assessment, developed by the author and commercially available, may be utilized as a tool to structure the interview process. This inventory has also been helpful in addressing denial and minimization issues in the early stages of treatment. Use of the Violence Inventory-Lethality

Assessment covers the seven factors listed above as well as other data. This in itself should begin to give the counselor a fair idea as to the degree of danger. Two of the above lethality categories involve chemical dependency issues. Therefore, it is crucial that counselors also be familiar with the drug and alcohol assessment process and be prepared to make the appropriate referrals should they be needed. Assessment of violence should at a minimum include descriptions of:

- All types of perpetrated violence

- Frequency of violent acts over past two years

- Threats to kill

- All other threats

- Most lethally perpetrated violence

- Most recent violence

- Prior attempts to kill

- Threats made towards friends and family members

- Violence perpetrated towards friends and family members

- Violence perpetrated outside the home

The same information from the victim's perspective would be critical to making a final determination of suitability for your program. Abusers commonly minimize the frequency and severity of their violent behavior even with the best of interviewers; therefore, a similar, thorough interview with the victim is necessary in order to make an informed decision regarding a particular abuser's suitability for an outpatient, less-structured program.

Finally, it is also important to procure the appropriate authorizations to release information in order to consult with all current and past medical and mental health professionals. Because aggression and violence are often chronic problems, these contacts could yield useful information about the client's history of violence as well as help clinicians accurately assess the client's current potential for violence (Monahan, 1993).

In addition to completing an alcohol/drug assessment, the Violence Inventory-Lethality Assessment examines a number of other issues the counselor may want to cover during the assessment process.

The proximity of the victim and offender. Is there currently a court stay-away or restraining order in place mandating that the perpetrator not have contact with his partner? If this is the case, does the offender work or live near the victim so that he can easily keep track of her whereabouts? Do the victim and offender work for the same company or in the same building? Is the victim currently residing at a shelter for battered women? Is the perpetrator likely to try to communicate through common friends, family, and in-laws? As a rule, the more overlap in their lives, the more difficult it may be for the offender to stay away from his partner if that is being required by the court. Not all victims have procured a restraining or stay-away order, but they may nevertheless want a physical separation from their partner. Separation and divorce in general is a time of high lethality, particularly if there is another man in the picture. However, many batterers have jealous ideation even if their partner is not involved with another man.

Current life stresses/crises. What other stresses is the offender experiencing, such as unemployment, physical illness or disability, recent death of a family member or friend, extremely stressful occupation, recent loss of job, poverty, etc.? These problems in conjunction with marital discord or separation may overwhelm the abuser to the point that he is operating under reduced emotional resources. When an individual is experiencing extreme stress he becomes extremely focused on struggling with the stressor, which may leave him with fewer psychological resources to cope with marital stress, a separation or court action. Often when under extreme stress, persons will look for areas to take control of in their lives. Reclaiming their relationship if they are separated, or other forms of acting out, may be perceived as one way of taking this control. In some cases, incarceration or other restrictions may be placed upon an abuser until the various crises resolve or subside.

Psychiatric diagnosis/history. Recent studies have indicated that psychiatric disorders increase the risk of violent behavior (Monahan, 1992). Therefore it is important that the counselor's assessment include a psychiatric diagnosis. Some offenders, specifically those with an affective disorder such as major depression, dythymia, cyclothymia, and bipolar disorder, may not be candidates for your program without being simultaneously on medication. Certain individuals suffering from personality disorders may benefit from adjunctive individual therapy. Men diagnosed with antisocial personality disorder are not likely to benefit from treatment of any kind. Some men who either were severely abused as children or experienced head injuries in the past may also need to be evaluated for medication, without which they are not likely to succeed in a counseling program. After a mental status exam is conducted, it may be apparent that the abuser is too emotionally overwhelmed to manage his behavior without more limitations upon his freedom.

The five-axis DSM-IV system (American Psychiatric Association, 1994) includes on Axis IV a description of psychosocial and environmental stressors such as problems with primary support group, problems related to social environment, educational problems, occupational problems, housing problems, economic problems, problems with access to health care services, problems related to interaction with the legal system/crime, and other psychosocial and environmental problems.

On Axis V, a Global Assessment of Functioning Scale examines the client's level of cognitive, emotional, and behavioral functioning ranging from very low (persistent danger of severely hurting self or others, persistent inability to maintain minimal personal hygiene, or serious suicidal act with clear expectation of death), to moderate (serious symptoms or any serious impairment in social, occupational, or school functioning), to high (superior functioning in a wide range of activities, life's problems never seem to get out of hand, is sought out by others because of his or her many positive qualities. No symptoms.).

These two scales are very useful in that they are behaviorally oriented, and regardless of the ultimate diagnosis, they clearly describe the number of stressors present in a client's life and the level of adaptation the client has attained in an effort to cope with those stressors. Counselors should also obtain the necessary authorizations to review prior mental health records, and consult with all current and previous medical/mental health professionals whom the client has seen.

Weapons in the home or accessible. Studies indicate that many murders in the home could be prevented were a weapon not easily accessible. Participation in any treatment program must be contingent on the removal of weapons, and on the production of secondary verification of their secure placement with others.

Previous criminal history. This information indicates the extent to which antisocial activity is present in an abuser's life. Generally, the more evidence of disregard for the rights of others, and others' property, the less likely the individual will benefit from counseling. This is particularly true if past criminal history involves violations of probation, parole, or such court orders as temporary restraining orders. Not all criminal history results in an arrest, and therefore incidents sometimes are not documented. Interviews with the victim, as opposed to the abuser, are more likely to acquire this type of information.

Attitudes towards violence. Many male batterers genuinely feel remorse about their violent behavior. However, many others believe that they are justified in using violence against their partner and therefore may not be good candidates for this program. Although some men may initially appear remorseful or self-righteous, counselors should not make a premature decision about motivation for treatment solely based on initial statements about their situation. Attitudes are more accurately evaluated by other factors, such as cooperation in the interview process, demonstration of appropriate affect, consistency of statements, honesty about history of violence as corroborated by the partner, and overall assessment and diagnosis.

Abuser motivation for change. Client motivation is very difficult to accurately assess, and in most cases is ultimately determined by participation in treatment and treatment outcome. However, given the general lethality of family violence, a mistake in accurately assessing this issue can result in a loss of life. Therefore it is imperative for counselors to pay particular attention to factors discussed in the previous paragraph in assessing whether or not an abuser is genuinely interested in changing his behavior. Many counselors like to believe they can help everyone who steps into their office. We know from experience, however, that many batterers continue to reoffend even when participating in the best treatment programs. For various reasons, ranging from psychiatric or neurological impairment to needing to "hit bottom," many batterers will not benefit from treatment and may need to be subjected to other sanctions that simply serve to protect the victim and the rest of society from their actions.

Victim dating or romantically involved with another person. Many male batterers experience feelings of extreme jealousy as their partners begin to withdraw either sexually or emotionally. They frequently accuse their partner of looking at, flirting with, or spending time with other men — even if there is no real basis for these beliefs. However, when a woman does start to develop intimate relationships with others, either before or subsequent to a separation, she may find herself at a particularly high risk of violence.

Many male batterers feel extremely threatened by other men or women receiving the intimate attention of their partner. These men are at great risk of emotional reactivity and acting out their impulses to make contact with their partner. The purpose of the contact may range from convincing her to stop the new relationship and reconcile with him, or worse, to seek revenge for the pain he perceives her as causing him. A thorough evaluation of this issue is necessary to determine who is and who is not at risk for violence. This is particularly true if specific threats of violence have been made with regard to this partner or others with whom she may be involved.

Personal/group evaluation. Lastly, experienced counselors may develop an intuitive feeling or sense about a particular abuser and for that reason alone may feel uncomfortable with his participation in their program. Because of the complexity of both the individual and marital dynamics of family violence, decisions regarding suitability for counseling should be made by a team of professionals. If this is not possible, private counselors are encouraged to consult with colleagues on a regular basis so as to better recognize high-risk cases and respond to crises.

CONTACT WITH THE VICTIM

It is important for counselors working with male batterers to contact the victim in order to receive corroborative data on the history of violence, alcohol and drug abuse, and other relevant factors related to lethality. In addition, throughout the offender's participation in treatment, the counselor should maintain regular contact with the victim in order to determine if the perpetrator is utilizing the educational material in an appropriate manner in his relationship. It is recommended that the counselor maintain weekly phone contact with partners and in-person contact with victims at least once every eight weeks. The informed consent form used by Learning to Live without Violence requires contact with the partners of all program participants. This also includes new relationships started after the man enters into counseling. Clients are encouraged to tell new emotional involvements about their history of domestic violence. Doing so, although it involves risking the new relationship, indicates a commitment to maintaining a violence-free life. Additionally, the program must have contact with new partners because, theoretically, the counselor is in a position of increased liability should a client perpetrate lethal violence towards a new partner. (See discussion of liability on p. 65.) In addition to partner follow-up, contact with other counselors involved with the perpetrator and/or victim is also recommended so that the counselors are working together and not giving opposing messages to family members.

THE BOTTOM LINE: WHO DO YOU WORK WITH AND HOW?

I have counseled male batterers in different settings (private practice, nonprofits, military, prison, etc.), with differing populations (inpatient vs. outpatient, court-referred vs. self-referred, monocultural vs. multicultural, civilian vs. military, etc.), and in differing treatment modalities (individual, group, and family). I have found that my screening criteria and overall counseling approach differ depending on each situation. All counselors are going to have their own preferences as to who they ultimately work with best. Some will only work with men who have demonstrated the most minimal violence in the past. Other professionals enjoy working with high-risk cases. In either case, it is important to think of domestic violence treatment as a long-term process that may begin with one form of counseling and evolve into other modalities over a period of years. Different approaches may be more effective with different types of perpetrators; therefore, evaluation is a key to becoming accurate at matching particular types of clients with your personal needs and your particular type of approach.

The development of a comprehensive treatment plan is important when working with male batterers for several reasons. The plan gives the client (and counselor) a structure that clearly defines the goals of treatment and how those goals will be achieved. Because of their lack of familiarity with counseling, many men will feel secure knowing that they will not be in treatment forever and that the expectations of successful completion are clear right from the start. Another reason for the treatment plan is for the counselor to keep focused on the primary identified goal of stopping violence and to not get sidetracked on other, and sometimes more interesting, topics. This is particularly important during the early stages of treatment, when helping men learn to control their violent impulses is of primary importance. Because these clients often present a variety of problems and complaints, treatment goals may be prioritized so clients understand that different issues will be addressed at different stages of treatment. In this way, for example, a man will not enter into counseling thinking that he will be immediately addressing divorce issues and therefore feel that he doesn't have to talk about his violence because he is no longer with his partner. It is also crucial that the treatment plan contain collateral referrals necessary for successful violence treatment (e.g., alcohol and drug treatment).

Of course, an indispensable part of any counseling program for male batterers is for the man to buy into the plan. This goal is as much a part of the art of counseling as it is the science. Developing positive rapport is important with any counseling client, but particularly important and difficult with male batterers. Many of these men hold the view that asking for help is tantamount to admitting weakness and therefore being less of a man. Because of the history that many male batterers have had with abusive and domineering fathers (and mothers), the client is likely to enter into counseling with a great deal of distrust for the process. He is not likely to want to make himself vulnerable to another who is perceived as having power over him (especially if he has been referred by the criminal justice system). Because of these issues alone, it is crucial that counselors approach their work with male batterers with genuine sensitivity and empathy so that positive rapport is possible. Counselors with unresolved feelings about their own family abuse are likely to either displace hostility toward their client or collude with their minimization and denial. Having a personal history of childhood abuse or family violence can certainly be an asset when working with male batterers, but when the counselor's psychological issues are left unchecked, those experiences can become a detriment to effective treatment. It is recommended that persons who experienced abuse as a child participate in their own counseling while working with male batterers so that their personal issues do not get confused with the psychological material presented by the client.

Below is a sample treatment plan for a man entering the Learning to Live without Violence Program (with the assumption that rapport has already been established and you have a relatively willing client open to the idea that counseling can help him with his problem).

Treatment Plan for John Smith

Intake: 11/4/94

Assessment sessions: 11/7, 14, 21, 28

Referred for alcohol and drug assessment: 11/21/94

Recommendation: 12-step program, 90 meetings in 90 days — then reevaluate for further treatment

Relationship status: Living together

Partner follow-up: Once/week — before session

Couples follow-up: Once every 6–8 weeks (partner agrees to participate in program)

Contact with partner's therapist: First week of each month (releases secured)

Stage 1 (Weeks 1–12)

Goals	Interventions
Integrate into group	Group building exercises — violence history
Prevent further violence	Time-outs
Learn definitions of violence	Lecture, group discussion
Identify violence patterns in relationship	Lecture, violence inventory
Identify cycle of violence	Lecture, cycle of violence exercise
Learn to identify and communicate anger	Anger management skill training
Learn to control escalation of emotions	Cognitive therapy — anger journal
Understand causes of domestic violence	Education, lecture, group discussions
Understand effects of domestic violence	Education, lecture, group discussions

Stage 2 (Weeks 13–24)

Goals	Interventions
Reinforce Stage 1 goals	Stage 1 interventions
Develop control over psychological abuse	Lecture, group discussion — violence inventory
Develop control over alcohol & drug use	Self-assessment, lecture, group discussion
Develop listening skills	Lecture — behavioral interventions
Identify & communicate other feelings	Lecture — feelings journal
Develop assertiveness skills	Reading, lecture — behavioral interventions
Learn stress reduction skills	Lecture — relaxation exercises

Stage 3 (Weeks 25–36)

Goals	Interventions
Reinforce Stage 1 & 2 goals	Stage 1 & 2 interventions
Identify emotional effects of childhood abuse	Lecture, group process — use previous cognitive/behavioral interventions to manage emotions
Identify cognitive effects of childhood abuse	Cognitive interventions — thought journal
Identify effects of childhood abuse on interpersonal relationships	Lecture, group discussion, attachment measures

PROTECT YOURSELF!

No matter what population of perpetrators a counselor may work with (high or low risk), she or he is likely to encounter homicidal or suicidal situations, and therefore it is crucial that counselors/programs institute the safeguards that are necessary to respond to high-risk crises. These safeguards include a security plan for home and offices, a good working relationship with local law enforcement agencies (police and prosecutors), coordination with local victims services (shelters, counseling programs, advocacy programs), on-call consulting mental health professionals, and advanced training in crisis management.

Because of the high risk that domestic violence clients present to clinicians, liability insurance is highly recommended. Familiarity with the laws relating to confidentiality, child and elder/adult dependent abuse, and dangerous situations is a must for counselors working with domestic violence cases. Lastly, it would be wise to include a statement to clients and their partners informing them of the limits of treatment. Although some studies have indicated a high remission rate of violent behavior while the perpetrator is in treatment and for some time afterwards, many men do continue to reoffend even while participating in highly effective treatment programs. Therefore, a specific statement to both parties will communicate the seriousness of the domestic violence while at the same time present a sobering statement about the real chance that violence will continue and may become more serious over time. Below is an example of such a statement.

A Message to Our Clients

The problem of domestic violence has received considerable attention in the past few years. Counseling programs for male batterers, and programs such as Learning to Live without Violence, have become increasingly available to men. However, because of the high lethality associated with domestic violence, even when men go into counseling, there continues to exist a real and present risk for continued violence.

The techniques you will learn in counseling are meant to help you learn how to identify and communicate your emotions in an appropriate manner, and how to change attitudes, both of which ultimately help to prevent violent behavior. However, we cannot guarantee that every man will stop his violent behavior. Many men have continued their violence while participating in the treatment programs. Therefore both victims and perpetrators must not be lulled into a false sense of security simply because they are in counseling. Individuals who have a problem with violence need long-term counseling in order to break those patterns. Some men do not change because they're simply not emotionally motivated to change. Other men may genuinely want to stop their violence but are prone to setbacks. Certain men are in need of a more intensive treatment plan over and above once-a-week sessions. A few, but a significant number, of men may ultimately need an inpatient, hospital-based program or jail if they are unable to effectively utilize once-a-week counseling in a constructive manner.

You may decide that the Learning to Live without Violence Program is not for you. If that is the case, we encourage you to seek out another program immediately. The longer you go without counseling, the greater the risk for continued violence. The greater the risk for violence, the greater the possibility that counseling will no longer be an option — instead, incarceration may be the only choice. Therefore, if you decide to leave our program, we recommend that you continue to attend sessions until you are ready to enter into another counseling situation so there is a minimal amount of time that passes between programs.

REFERENCES

American Psychiatric Association (1994). *Diagnostic and statistical manual of mental disorders: Fourth edition (DSM-IV)*. Washington, DC: American Psychiatric Association.

Browne, A. (1987). *When battered women kill*. New York: Free Press.

Monahan, J. (1992). Mental disorder and violent behavior: Perceptions and evidence. *American Psychologist*, April, v47 (4), 511-521.

Monahan, J. (1993). Limiting therapist exposure to Tarasoff liability: Guidelines for risk containment. *American Psychologist*, Mar., v48 (3), 242-250.

CHAPTER FIVE

Using *Learning to Live without Violence:* An Introduction

Before discussing how to use the *Learning to Live without Violence* workbook in counseling, it is important to consider what treatment modality will be utilized (individual or group counseling) and who will be doing the counseling. In addition, if group counseling is the modality of choice, then a further decision needs to be made as to whether the groups are to be short- or long-term in length, educational or therapeutic in nature, and open-ended or closed with regard to the admission of new members.

INDIVIDUAL VS. COUPLES VS. GROUP COUNSELING

Learning to Live without Violence, although it may be utilized with individuals and couples, was written with the assumption that most programs will be working with abusers in a group setting. This is because once programs start up, there is usually a continual stream of referrals; therefore, one or two individual counselors cannot handle that many cases. However, in settings such as rural areas, where referrals of perpetrators are few and far between, individual and couples counseling may be a more practical approach to working with domestic violence. In addition to these reasons, specific ethnic/cultural populations may be more amenable to individual, couples, or family therapy as opposed to group counseling. Counselors need to assess this issue based on their experience and knowledge of those specific ethnic groups.

Individual counseling with male batterers will be more process-oriented than in a group setting, and therefore the relationship between the counselor and client will become more instrumental to the client's accepting and utilizing the specific interventions. For some men, individual counseling may be experienced as extremely threatening. The counselor must take special care so as to maximize the prospect of a successful treatment outcome. In these cases, counselors and clients may both find the experience very frustrating unless the counselor clinically addresses these process issues. Men whose father or mother was particularly authoritarian may negatively react to a counselor who approaches the sessions in a harsh, dogmatic, or controlling fashion. The development of good rapport and a positive relationship will be vital to the client cooperation in any modality of counseling. The counselor must be firm and clear about boundaries and limits, but more support may be necessary to create a sense of openness with the client.

Men who come from particularly violent families may have developed a withdrawn, fearful, or extremely introverted way of interacting with others. Individual counseling may be experienced as overwhelming, demanding more interaction than the client is normally comfortable with. In this situation, along with positive rapport and trust, the counselor must be extremely patient with long silences and not demand more from the client than he can give.

Lastly, not all abusers have the verbal skills, self-knowledge, or education to feel comfortable with such an intense form of interaction as individual counseling. Therefore, a counselor needs to meet the client at his level of sophistication rather than have unrealistic expectations about the client's accessibility to the material. Individual sessions may simply be focused on helping the man get through a difficult period and imparting specific skills for handling conflict at home, rather than meeting an unrealistic agenda or achieving changes in character structure.

For the clients who can handle individual counseling, the sessions may focus on education on domestic violence, or specific behavioral interventions addressing violent behavior, or understanding the historical antecedents of today's problems. However, counselors should be prepared for the possibility that for some individuals, one-on-one counseling may be threatening or overwhelming; therefore, counselors may need to be flexible in the manner they use the workbook or how quickly they address various clinical issues. Some counselors require the client to read the book with the intention of discussing specific homework in the session. Other counselors will simply recommend the book and talk about it only if the client chooses to bring it up for discussion.

Couples counseling and family therapy may also be effective ways of addressing domestic violence; however, it is beyond the scope of this book to explore how to specifically adapt the material in *Learning to Live without Violence* in those modalities. The main concern about couples and family therapy, voiced by activists in the domestic violence movement, is that these modalities can either accidentally or purposefully give the message to both the man and the woman that she, the victim, is in part responsible for the violence of the man. Although some systems-oriented therapists believe this to be true, many couples and family therapists can walk the fine line by working with the system or interaction and not blaming the victim for the violence. Even in cases of mutual battering, both members of the couple can be given the message that violence is their responsibility and that, outside of legal self-defense, there is no justification for its use.

As mentioned earlier, couples and family therapy may be preferable over group or individual counseling with members of certain cultural groups that place a heavy value on family assistance in problem-solving. Many men who are not involved with the criminal justice system will go to counseling only if their wives go along. Therefore, couples counseling may be the only alternative for these individuals if the wife is not willing to leave the relationship. Family therapy also has the advantage that all the family members are able to talk about how the violence has affected their relationships with one another. It may be an excellent way for the perpetrator to clearly understand how his violence has not only affected his partner, but his children as well. These sessions, like a drug or alcohol family intervention, can be very effective in motivating the batterer to take a hard and serious look at his behavior.

In the group setting, peer support and pressure encourages men to make and maintain the necessary changes to control violent impulses. This is one of the strongest arguments for group treatment. Feedback from men who have personally experienced domestic violence often can help to break the veneer of denial that so many men present at the beginning of treatment. Peer batterers are also often the best salesmen with regard to the behavioral techniques presented in the program. Similarly, fellow group members are able to provide important peer support and assistance during times of crisis as well as in the early stages of treatment.

Process groups may consist of as few as four offenders and one or two facilitators. Larger educational-oriented groups could consist of as many as fifteen or twenty men. The smaller the group, the more individual attention men receive and the easier it is to focus on group process. The larger the group, the less process-oriented and more educational in nature it becomes. It is encouraged that two facilitators lead each group so that administrative work, follow-up, and crisis-handling does not fall on one person's shoulders.

Over the years we have heard of counselors successfully using *Learning to Live without Violence* in group, individual, and couples counseling. Although the primary target of the book is men, women and children could also benefit from the educational material discussed. The material in *Learning to Live without Violence* is currently being adapted for work with children and adolescents who have difficulties with anger and/or violence.

OPEN VS. CLOSED GROUPS

Programs with a high volume of steady referrals are likely to regularly have clients in the assessment process and ready to start in group counseling. If this is the case for your program, you may consider having the groups be open-ended (having men join at any time) rather than closed (having men start together and end together). There are advantages and disadvantages to both situations. Let's explore both alternatives so that you may decide which option best fits your situation.

An advantage with closed groups, in which men start and end together, is that every man tells his story in the first session so that further time is not taken up with this issue in subsequent sessions. A bond between the men forms by the middle phase of the program and serves as encouragement for cooperation and commitment to change. This dynamic may happen to a lesser degree in open-ended groups.

An inevitable disadvantage to closed groups is that of attrition as a result of discharges due to reoffenses, or lack of motivation or participation. A small closed group of six men could dwindle down to three or four participants. Additionally, in closed groups men are all at similar levels of the change process and may reinforce each other's denial and lack of motivation. Furthermore, with a closed group new participants in the program may have to be seen individually or placed on hold for up to ten or eleven weeks before a group is available.

The *Learning to Live without Violence* workbook was written to accommodate open-ended groups, such that a man could join the group and either catch up, if the chapters have been sequentially covered, or work on the currently covered chapter. The primary anger-management material can be read while in the assessment process before entering the group. An advantage to open-ended groups is that new men can be inspired and encouraged by men who have already broken their denial and are utilizing the intervention techniques. Another advantage of the open-ended group is that staff time is not taken up with individual counseling sessions.

MALE VS. FEMALE COUNSELORS

There are no hard and fast rules about the issue of the counselor's gender. Programs across the country have utilized both male and/or female counselors to work with male batterers, and their success rate, in general, is often higher than the success rates with many other clinical populations. From our experience, the gender of the counselor is not as important as the counselor's attitudes about men, women, and victims and perpetrators of violence.

Counselors who work with male batterers must be able to incorporate a counseling style that is both confronting and yet caring, supportive, and encouraging. Many clients come from abusive families; as a result, their behavior and attitudes may pull for a rigid and controlling response from others. Over the years the client may have even grown to expect this response from others. However, counselors should be cautious to not act out the client's expectations of others or reenact the abusive dynamic that existed between the man and his abusive parent. On the other hand, counselors must feel comfortable setting limits, presenting consequences, and confronting destructive attitudes and behaviors in a direct, assertive, and caring manner.

Counselors of both genders will have to deal with intimidation, competitiveness, and resistance from male batterers. Male counselors may have to deal with men's homophobia, whereas female counselors may have to deal with men's attempts at seductiveness. How these are handled will depend on the counselor and the client. However, the counselor is encouraged to find an appropriate response to each situation rather than respond in rigid and predictable patterns that do not consider the client with whom he or she is interacting.

USING *LEARNING TO LIVE WITHOUT VIOLENCE* IN GROUPS

Learning to Live without Violence: A Handbook for Men was originally developed to be utilized in a short-term, educationally oriented group for male batterers. Early editions of the book had the chapter titles in the table of contents divided by weeks (Week 1, Week 2, etc.). This was primarily done to assist counselors in prioritizing material for their group sessions. For example, anger-management material was presented in the first three or four weeks, followed by other suggested interventions such as stress-reduction techniques, assertiveness training, and alcohol and drug issues.

When the first and several subsequent editions of *Learning to Live without Violence* were published, the majority of programs that were offering groups for male batterers were short-term in nature, usually less than twenty-four weeks. Over the years, many programs have lengthened their group durations because they have realized that treatment of violence must be a long-term process. Therefore, rather than place new clients on waiting lists, programs have begun instituting additional groups, all running simultaneously. The most recent edition of *Learning to Live without Violence* therefore simply lists the chapters in the table of contents and makes no reference to which chapters should be covered in what session. We wanted to let clinicians know that they can use the book in any length group and therefore may choose to focus on any one or several chapters for as many sessions as they wish. For example, a counselor in an inpatient chemical dependency program who is running a batterers group may feel that the alcohol and drug chapter warrants a long discussion and series of exercises over two or three sessions — even before addressing anger-management issues. In other words, counselors need to use the book in any way that makes sense to their approach to counseling male batterers.

SETTING RULES FOR GROUPS

An important part of counseling male batterers is helping them to set limits for themselves — to recognize that violence is unacceptable behavior and is not an option to solving interpersonal problems. Clear and firm group rules can set the tone for their learning to set limits with themselves. Group rules include information about confidentiality, attendance, anger and violence within the group, alcohol and drug use prior to session, and other expectations. Below is a list of possible rules that you may want to add to or alter.

- Do not interrupt when people are talking.

- No advice-giving — talk about your feelings.

- Start on time.

- End on time.

- No touching without permission from others.

- No alcohol or drugs twenty-four hours before group.

- No eating or drinking during sessions.

- Keep the focus of conversation on anger and violence (or the chapter of the week).

- Keep to the structure of the group.

- Be honest.

It is also important for men to know that what is discussed in the group is confidential. That means that men should not even talk with their partners about something one of the men has said in the group. The intention may be to talk about general issues, but in discussing specifics he may inadvertently reveal a member's identity.

CHECK-IN PROCESS

Before discussing the specific educational material planned for a session, it is important that any new man should introduce himself by openly discussing his history of violence with fellow group members. This exercise reiterates the purpose of the group — to stop violence

— and also continues with the process of breaking the denial and minimization of problems that many men experience in varying degrees. Typically with closed groups, this process would occur at the first group meeting and, in open-ended groups, whenever a new man joins. In either case, participants are encouraged to ask questions and confront denial, minimization, and externalization (blaming). In open-ended groups, when new members may only join periodically, older members may briefly introduce themselves by discussing their past violent behaviors and what they have learned by participating in the program. A new member may also be assigned a "buddy" or "sponsor," a person who has already been in the program for a minimum period of time, to help orient them to the material and serve as a general source of support. In each subsequent meeting, men will participate in the check-in procedure so that they continually review their progress in the program.

At the beginning of each group session, each member needs to briefly discuss the highlights of his week. This is called the *group check-in*. It is completed by answering the questions listed below. In this way the group leaders or facilitators will know how each man is progressing in the program. After the check-in, persons who perpetrated violence in the past week, those who are having difficulty utilizing the anger-management material, or those who are in crisis, have the opportunity to discuss their situation and receive group support in changing their patterns.

Group Check-in

- Did you perpetrate physical, sexual, property or psychological violence this week?

- How many real time-outs did you take this week?

- How many practice time-outs did you take this week?

- How many times did you get angry when you might have taken a time-out, but didn't? What did you do instead?

- Are there any important issues you need to discuss in the session today?

After the group check-in, the men who perpetrated violence need to discuss their situation first. In doing so they should try to address the following questions:

Processing Acts of Violence

- What violence did you perpetrate? What specifically did you do?

- When did you notice you were becoming angry? How did you know you were angry?

- When could you have chosen to act in another way? What might have been another way of dealing with the situation?

- What is your plan of action for the next week? What can you do to lessen the chance of another incidence of violence?

Each man must develop a plan of action to avoid another incident. This plan may include finding an individual counselor, attending AA or another chemical abuse program, separating, taking a practice time-out every day, and/or reading and completing the exercises in a particular chapter in this workbook. Whatever the plan, it should involve specific, observable behaviors. Vague or general statements such as, "I'll try harder," or "I'll never do it again," or "I'll just stop it," are hard to hold to and don't set up markers for measuring improvement. Interventions, as a rule, should be behavioral in nature so as to best measure their effectiveness.

Next (or at the beginning if no men have been violent in the past week), attention should turn to those men in crisis and at risk for violence, or who have not been utilizing the anger-management material. The assumption of the program is that only through weekly rehearsals or practice will men be able to easily utilize the anger-management material when it is truly needed — during a conflict with their partner. Resistance to utilizing the anger-management material is discussed in a subsequent section of this chapter.

GROUP STRUCTURE

As indicated in Chapter Four, the group rules are clearly defined to the client at the onset of treatment. Likewise, the check-in procedure described above should also be explained to the client either during the assessment process or at the first group session attended. This structured format is key to the success of the Learning to Live without Violence Program. The structure helps to keep the focus of the groups on violence prevention as well as modeling for the clients the importance of self-control, order, and predictability. Within each group session, sufficient time may be set aside to deal with specific issues, other than the education material, of importance to the participants. In this way each meeting will be similar and also different depending on the issues the participants are confronting during the intervening weeks.

The group facilitators are actively engaged in the educational and therapeutic process. They should also, however, encourage participants to present information, share homework assignments, and disclose personal information relevant to the material being discussed. If group members are not confronting one another on their minimization and denial (which is not uncommon in the early stages of the group development), the group leaders should encourage this in the clients ("Does anyone hear John minimizing his violence?" "How can you relate to that behavior pattern?"). Leaders may also demonstrate the sensitive use of direct confrontation ("It sounds to me that you are minimizing the seriousness of your violence."). In these ways group leaders encourage participation and interaction between clients and at the same time may serve as role models to group members.

INTRODUCING NEW MEMBERS TO THE GROUP

In open-ended groups, new members are likely to join along the way and need to be integrated into an already existing group dynamic. One way to facilitate this transition is to encourage the new member to share his situation much as other members may have done at the first group meeting. Below are a number of suggested questions:

- What was the situation that brought you to this group?

- How long have you been physically, sexually, or psychologically violent?

- Describe your most recent incidence of violence.

- Describe how you were physically, sexually, or psychologically violent.

- Describe your most lethal act of violence.

- How has your violence affected your partner? Your children?

- Why do you think you are violent?

- What are you looking to receive from this group?

- How will you know you got it?

After the new member introduces himself, the rest of the group may want to also answer several of the same questions. After this process, new members are likely to feel somewhat more comfortable in this new and unusual setting. Another way to help men become oriented to the group process, as mentioned before, is by assigning new members with a buddy, similar to an AA sponsor, who will be available between sessions in case of an emergency and who will help familiarize him to the experience of being in a batterers group.

CHAPTER ONE — DEFINITIONS OF VIOLENCE

The first chapter of *Learning to Live without Violence* is the important introductory material that sets the frame for counseling. The definitions of violence and the explanation of the time-out procedure help men to clearly define what behaviors they are trying to change and the primary technique they will utilize to reach that goal. During this session, group leaders may encourage participants to brainstorm the definitions of physical, sexual, and psychological violence. Encourage them to be specific, using observable behaviors as indicators. *Learning to Live without Violence* uses general definitions with a few examples. After the brainstorming exercise, counselor may fill in the missing behaviors by using the list of violent acts below.

- **Physical violence** includes hitting, burning, biting, spitting, clawing, scratching, tying up with rope or other materials, being forced to eat nonedible food or materials, hanging, drowning, slapping, holding, grabbing, shoving, pushing, kicking, choking, scratching, punching, pulling, pinching, pulling hair, twisting arm, restraining, holding, threatening and hitting with weapons or objects.

- **Sexual violence** includes physically forcing or coercing one's partner to have fondling of breasts or genitals, sexual intercourse, oral sex, sodomy, sex with animals, forcing a person to have sexual intercourse or sexual activity with another person, masturbation, forced sexual activity with objects.

- **Property violence** includes throwing, breaking, and kicking things, pounding a fist through a window or wall, tearing up clothes, physically abusing a pet or other animals.

- **Psychological violence** includes all threats of violence, including threats to hit, threats to sexually assault, and threats to kill. Counselors may decide to use the **Amnesty International** definition of psychological violence (see earlier discussion of the definitions of psychological violence), which would include **isolation** (e.g., not letting her socialize with friends or family members, forcing her to stay at home with you all the time or not letting her leave the house without you, not letting her use the car or learn to drive, and moving away from all her support systems, such as friends or family members), **induced debility-producing exhaustion** (e.g., keeping her up all night during a fight, waking her up to argue with her or physically or sexually abuse her, making her do all the work at home, forcing her into a servant role, keeping her pregnant, or not allowing her to have support in taking care of the children), **monopolization of perceptions** (e.g., pathological jealousy, having to know where she is all the time or who she is with, accusing her of being with other men, looking at other men or wanting to be with other men, following her, controlling finances so she cannot leave, stalking her after a separation or divorce, refusing to obey restraining orders), **threats** (e.g., threats to kill the victim or others, threats of suicide, threats to kidnap children), **mental degradation** (e.g., name-calling, denying the victim's power, telling her she is crazy, trying to convince her that she is insane through the use of altered states of consciousness), **alcohol or drug use** (force and encouragement of use), and **occasional indulgences** (e.g., promises to stop the violence or get counseling, gift-giving, and display of sensitivity and tolerance to manipulate forgiveness).

UTILIZING THE TIME-OUT: TECHNIQUE AND RESISTANCES

In addition to defining violence, introducing men to the time-out technique is critical in the early stages of treatment. Typically, men are given a copy of the workbook on the first assessment visit and instructed to read the first chapter. The time-out procedure is explained to clients at the first assessment appointment. They are instructed to immediately take "practice time-outs" so as to get used to walking away from a conflict situation. Although time-outs are easy in theory, in practice, for many men, they can be quite difficult.

Time-outs are hard to do because men grow up believing that only a coward will walk away from a fight. For most men, the initial impulse is to stay and finish it, or at least get in the last word. Counselors should encourage men to consider this issue by discussing the feelings they might experience in taking a time-out. Feelings of shame, embarrassment, and guilt can cause a man either to not think about walking away or to resist doing so.

Another reason it is difficult for men to take time-outs is because it may be hard to walk away from an argument that is unfinished. It may be very important for some men to resolve the issue at hand. Counselors may explain to men that unresolved issues happen all the time in relationships. It is better that an issue be unresolved than escalate into violence. Once tempers flare, conflicts are rarely resolved anyhow, until both parties have had the opportunity to calm down, think of constructive ways to solve the conflict, and be open to listening to the other person. It is important to remind men that their first goal is to stop violence and rebuild trust. Solving the original conflict may have to come at a later date after these initial goals have been met.

Many men have expressed the fear that their partners will be gone when they return. Similarly, women have feared that their partner will not return after his time-out. If the woman does not feel safe, she may be gone when he returns, but if he has taken a time-out, at least there will not have been any violence, which is the priority of the counseling program. It is strongly emphasized that men return at the promised time so that trust may begin to be reestablished in the relationship.

Another frequent problem men have with time-outs is staying away from alcohol and other drugs. Many men will have the impulse to anesthetize themselves to the anxiety and other feelings they experienced either during the conflict or as a result of having to take a time-out at all. Some men will go to a bar to hang out with their friends for support. It is important for counselors to emphasize that the time-out is a chance to calm down and think clearly in order to best solve the problem. Alcohol and other drugs obviously impede this process. The time-out procedure was originally conceived as a time for the men to be alone and not get support from others. The idea was that a man not talk with friends who might ultimately take his side and support his being self-righteous, defensive, and blaming of his partner. However, men may be encouraged to call fellow group members, who are more likely to see the value of supporting his calming down and not defensively reacting towards his partner. If group members have friends outside the program who support personal growth and the counseling program goals, there is no reason why they shouldn't call those friends in times of crisis or during time-outs. It is important that men understand that time-outs are not social time, but time to learn new ways of coping with anger and conflict in interpersonal relationships. Ultimately, men need to be encouraged to use the time-outs even if they feel their problem with violence has gone away or when they believe they are in control of their anger. It can be explained to the client that if he doesn't or can't take a time-out when he doesn't need one (feeling low-level anger), he's not likely to take one when he does need one (experiencing extreme anger)!

Occasionally, some men will refuse to take time-outs as they are prescribed by the group leaders. This situation needs to be quickly addressed, because men who refuse to take time-outs are at high risk for future violence. It is important to explore this problem directly with the men. Occasionally, women may resist their partner's taking time-outs and therefore may be overtly or covertly pressuring them to not use the technique. If this is the case, counselors may want to meet with the couple, discuss their concerns, and explore solutions. Another reason that men may refuse to take time-outs is because they either don't believe they are at risk for future violence or may be in denial altogether as to the seriousness of their problem. In any case, men who refuse to take time-outs are noncompliant with the treatment; therefore, counselors need to evaluate whether the client is suitable for the treatment program. Like the suicidal client who refuses medication or voluntary hospitalization, the male batterer who refuses to utilize behavioral techniques geared to prevent violence is at great risk for harming others — which in turn increases professional liability for the treating therapist.

Not all perpetrators are treatable. For some men, incarceration may be the only viable alternative. We have not yet found treatment interventions that will address the needs of all, or even most, male batterers. Therefore, counselors must realistically appraise the suitability of each client for their program, realizing that many men will not benefit either from their particular program or any known rehabilitation program for male batterers.

CHAPTER SIX

Cognitive and Behavioral Interventions

The first two chapters of *Learning to Live without Violence* address the time-out technique and much of the necessary educational material relating to domestic violence. Topics in these introductory chapters include the definition of violence, the sex-roles issue, effects of violence against women and children, legal issues, characteristics of male batterers, childhood abuse issues, relationship of alcohol and drugs to violence, the cycle of violence, power, and control in intimate relationships, sexuality and violence, and responsibility for violence. These topics all set the critical frame of keeping the focus of the groups on the cessation of all forms of violent behavior.

Chapter Three in the workbook discusses the issue of mandated counseling. This is important for most men in counseling groups, because the majority are not voluntary consumers of mental health services. Typically, men have been mandated by the courts, or in the case of the military by their commanding officer, into treatment programs. However, there are increasing numbers of men in counseling because their partner has already left or is threatening to leave if he doesn't receive professional counseling. Counselors will be dealing with issues relating to denial, minimization, and anger regarding forced counseling to one degree or another for much of the treatment process. This is particularly true in short-term (less than twelve months) treatment programs. Clients frequently portray themselves as victims of the system or not understood by others. However they present these patterns of denial and minimization, it is crucial to successful treatment that counselors address this issue from the onset, for as long as men see themselves as the victims they can never fully understand the seriousness of their problem with violence.

At some point, men who participate in programs on a long-term basis will make the personal decision to receive treatment for themselves as opposed to doing it for others. Even when individuals begin treatment against their will, over time they may become internally motivated to change their lives. Although counselor skills in confronting resistance play an important role in the breaking down of the batterer's defenses, challenges by peers seem to bring this process along much quicker than with an individual counseling situation. Other techniques that I have found helpful include showing the perpetrator pictures of his injured partner, copies of police reports or trial transcripts, and intervention-type sessions with family members confronting the batterer on his destructive behaviors.

One of the reasons most batterer programs have developed their orientation in the direction of education and cognitive-behavior group therapy is related to the lack of internal motivation for counseling that many men demonstrate. Educational and cognitive-behavioral interventions give structure to the process of psychotherapy, which for many men can otherwise be a confusing and diffuse experience. Men are typically not comfortable with talking about inner thoughts and feelings and may find psychodynamically oriented therapy awkward, uncomfortable, or threatening. Likewise, cognitive-behavioral interventions are thinking, rather than feeling, oriented. Because many men use their logic (thinking mode) to solve problems, they are likely to find cognitive-behavioral interventions to be concrete, logical, and fitting more easily into their world view. Lastly, men are often prone to succumb to peer pressure in groups, and are therefore more likely to open up if several of their peers do so in a counseling group. For these, and other reasons, many counselors have found cognitive-behavioral interventions quite effective with helping male batterers stop their violent behaviors.

COGNITIVE AND BEHAVIORAL INTERVENTIONS

Cognitive and behavioral theories provide the primary interventions used in the Learning to Live without Violence groups. Both theories are designed to be problem-focused and short-term in nature, which fits with many perpetrator treatment programs offered today.

The cognitive interventions help men learn to stop the dysfunctional thought patterns that only serve to escalate anxiety and other dysphoric mood states, which lead to acting out in the form of physical, sexual, or psychological violence. The behavioral interventions offer the man specific techniques to learn anger- and conflict-management skills, stress-reduction strategies, and assertiveness and communication skills. The educational material is interspersed throughout the program to augment the therapeutic techniques with insight into the causes and solutions to the problem of domestic violence.

The reason we believe that education is not sufficient to treat this problem comes in part from experience but, more importantly, from the ever-growing scientific literature on domestic violence, particularly about the male batterer. Although there are no definitive studies to date as to the psychological and social attributes of the male batterer, increasing numbers of studies indicate that men who batter do have emotional problems to one degree or another. These problems range from the more entrenched personality disorders (borderline, narcissistic, or antisocial) to the more easily treated chemical dependency or post-traumatic stress disorders. The notion that male batterers are just men acting like men is an inaccurate oversimplification of the problem that ultimately doesn't help in solving the issue of violence against women.

The most consistent risk factor that has been identified to date is exposure to violence as a child (Hotaling and Sugerman, 1986). The witnessing of domestic violence has been identified by scholars as one form of psychological maltreatment of children (Rosenberg, 1987; Goodman and Rosenberg, 1987). Research has indicated that this form of child abuse has as detrimental an effect on children as physical and sexual abuse. Since the majority of male batterers have witnessed marital violence, then as with other victims of psychological maltreatment, the violence they witnessed evidently had a profound effect on their developing psyche. If we were to track the females from these same families, it probably would not be surprising to find that a significant number have become involved with abusive relationships. The reality is that violence destroys the sense of safety, trust, and nurturance necessary for the development of healthy males and females in families.

For many of these men, intimate relationships cause great anxiety that is managed through a number of common ways. Some men manage their anxiety through violence. A build-up of anxiety is relieved by a violent episode which results in a pattern of self-reinforcing tension and release. Some men use alcohol and drugs as a way of managing their emotional stress and tension. Other men may also emotionally distance themselves from their partner as a means of coping with the anxiety of being rejected or feeling their self-esteem being attacked. No matter what mechanism they ultimately use to cope with the anxiety associated with intimacy, these men experience intimate relationships as being highly threatening and therefore approach marriage with a great deal of anxiety and fear.

The studies on male batterers are important for a number of reasons. First, they begin to conceptualize the psychological dynamics that contribute to violent behavior. Second, they may also help us understand the etiology of domestic violence — which may ultimately help us identify who is at risk and how to prevent violence with high-risk children in the first place. Lastly, researchers are beginning to bring together a number of distinct disciplines within psychology that give meaning to the notion of interdisciplinary studies: developmental psychology, attachment theory, psychological maltreatment of children, trauma theory, and domestic violence research.

COGNITIVE THEORY AS IT APPLIES TO TREATMENT OF MALE BATTERERS

According to cognitive-therapy theory, beliefs about one's self, others, and situations greatly contribute to affective responses and ultimately to behaviors. Cognitive interventions proposed in *Learning to Live without Violence* are specifically directed towards maladaptive thinking processes that serve to escalate anxiety and anger, and produce the need to control the partner as a means to quell emotional dysphoria. These interventions are geared toward teaching men how to soothe their own feelings that result from this escalation process rather than looking to external factors (their partner). In *Learning to Live without Violence*, the maladaptive thought patterns are divided into two common patterns that we have found batterers utilize to cope with conflictual situations: denial and minimization (stuffing) and externalization (escalating).

Denial and minimization cognition patterns or thoughts ultimately contribute to violent patterns because, in their most basic form, the man is denying or is unaware of having any negative feelings at all. Other forms of this type of thought patterns include beliefs that one is unworthy and therefore doesn't have the right to get angry, and a lack in confidence that the man can handle the conflict which may ensue after expressing controversial emotions. These beliefs and thought patterns can lead to explosive behaviors when the emotional stress becomes too much as a result of lack of communication. Typical thought patterns of this type include:

- "I'm not angry" (denial).

- "It's no big deal" (minimization).

- "I don't have the right to be angry" (low self-esteem).

- "If I tell her how I feel, it's going to lead to a fight" (lack of confidence).

For many men growing up in violent homes, anger was a dangerous emotion. Later, as adults, these persons shy away from conflict or situations that may elicit "negative" emotions. To say that most batterers have an easy time expressing their anger is simply not correct. Many of these men have trouble expressing any emotion — anger or any other emotion. Over time denial and minimization of feelings lead to explosions for obvious reasons. Therefore, many of the behavioral interventions focus on awareness and communication of anger and other feelings. In addition to denying their own emotional responses to situations, batterers also tend to be self-critical and therefore question the justification of their feeling response to their partner. One may say that batterers who "stuff" their feelings are unaware of their emotional responses to situations, or they may be aware of their feelings but lack the self-esteem that their emotions are valid and the self-confidence that they possess the skills to appropriately express themselves and consequently deal with the responses of others.

Externalization cognition patterns or thoughts contribute to violent patterns of behavior because they ultimately increase arousal, justify defensiveness, and locate the focus of control on others rather than the self. Typical are thought patterns reflecting a belief that the other person is responsible for the man's emotional reactions. In *Learning to Live without Violence,* this externalizing pattern is referred to as *escalating* and primarily defined as blaming. In their most benign forms, these thoughts consist of the belief that the other person is making him feel uncomfortable. In their more severe form these thoughts may manifest as paranoid ideation, perceiving the other as evil or wicked, and obsessive thought patterns.

One goal of *Learning to Live without Violence* is to help men learn to "direct" their feelings rather than minimize, deny, or externalize them. *Directing* is defined as making an "I" statement followed by an expression of emotion (e.g., "I'm feeling angry.") and ideally, a statement of cause (e.g., "You called me incompetent in front of my boss."). The primary purpose is that "directing" is generally considered good communication. The "directing" statement does not encourage denial or minimization of emotions. In addition, this type of statement, if done correctly, will begin to move the batterer's focus of control from his partner to himself. Another purpose of this intervention is to help men learn to self-soothe, a skill that many have not learned before, particularly if they grew up in a violent home.

BEHAVIORAL INTERVENTIONS

As indicated in the previous chapter, the time-out technique is the primary intervention utilized in the Learning to Live without Violence Program. The "anger journal" is the second most important intervention in this program. This exercise is prescribed to the batterers in order for them to become more aware of their thought patterns and how they ultimately affect their emotions, such as anger, and behaviors, such as aggression. The anger journal is to be completed whenever a man feels any level of anger, frustration, or uncomfortable affect. Specific questions include:

- What were the physical signs of the anger?

- What were the behavioral signs of the anger?

- Did he take a time-out?

- Did he "stuff" his anger?

- Did he escalate his anger?

- Did he direct his anger?

- What type of "I" statements did he make to himself or his partner?

- What physical activity did he use on his time-out?

- Was he under the influence of alcohol or drugs at the time?

Ideally, the anger journal should be used daily; however, two entries are included after each chapter in the workbook. Counselors are encouraged to require participants to complete at least two entries between sessions. Clients can share one or two of their entries each week in group.

Another important behavioral intervention is provided by the anger-sensitization exercises. These help the client learn to identify the physical (body) responses and their behavioral (action) responses to anger and other forms of arousal. The goal of these interventions is to help men learn to identify their anger while it is manageable, before the level of emotion reaches the point when it is difficult to control. The anger-sensitization exercises, the anger journal, and the time-out technique form the basic triad of interventions for the Learning to Live without Violence Program.

WHY THE FOCUS ON ANGER?

Theoretically, one goal of treatment is to have men become more aware of and appropriately communicate all feelings. However, the reason for the immediate focus on anger is because violence often occurs when men experience this type of affect. Furthermore, the focus of the program is on learning appropriate ways of communicating anger, managing conflict, and avoiding violence. Therefore, the focus on anger serves as a reminder of why men are in the program in the first place. When men become angry (whether or not they may also feel hurt), they are at risk of acting violent and therefore need to pay close attention to their arousal process and apply constructive methods of solving the situation at hand. In addition to stopping violence, other specific goals of the Learning to Live without Violence Program include the necessity to:

- Become aware of patterns of the use of alcohol and drugs and their relationship to violence

- Develop listening skills, particularly to the partner's anger regarding past violence

- Learn to identify and communicate other feelings besides anger

- Develop assertiveness skills — saying no and asking for what you want

- Develop stress-reduction skills

- Become aware of jealousy patterns as a form of psychological violence

- Handle emotional stress regarding separation and divorce

- Integrate skills learned in the group in the relationship with the partner

- Develop an attitude that recovery is an ongoing process

- Engage in individual, couple, or family therapy during or after the group program

- Develop empathy towards partner and children

- Develop awareness of sex-role attitudes and their relation to violence

- Develop awareness of the effects of childhood abuse on adult behavior

In addition to these specific goals, more general goals include:

- Decreasing isolation

- Developing an interpersonal support system

- Increasing feelings of self-control

- Increasing feelings of self-esteem

- Confronting minimization and denial of problems

- Increasing awareness of the danger of violent behavior

- Developing an awareness of the effects of violence on family members

- Accepting the consequences of behavior

- Increasing awareness of violence in society

- Continually assessing potential lethality

- Periodically assessing treatment effectiveness

- Supporting other therapeutic goals particular to individual client

These more-general goals can be achieved in a number of ways, but nevertheless should be incorporated into the program's educational curriculum or therapeutic interventions.

REASONS FOR TERMINATION FROM THE PROGRAM

As indicated earlier, not all programs, including Learning to Live without Violence, are going to meet all the needs of all the men who have problems with violence. Some men may do better in an educational program, whereas other men may excel in a psychotherapy program, and others somewhere in between. Certain men may not be ready for treatment for a variety of reasons, and therefore no program outside of incarceration may help them stop their violent behavior. Because of the potential lethality in domestic violence cases, counselors need to continually assess each client's progress in the program. They must be ready to make important treatment decisions that could indirectly affect the safety and well-being of these clients as well as family members. Because it is difficult to determine when a particular client is a treatment failure and when, on the other hand, there was a poor match between a particular treatment program and the client, counselors need to consider both options as possible reasons for the following problems.

The most common reasons for terminating treatment for male batterers are for multiple violent reoffenses, breaking group rules (e.g., confidentiality, aggressive acting-out in group, attending sessions under the influence of alcohol or drugs), poor participation (e.g., missed appointments, refusing to talk in group, refusing to complete assignments), and refusal to accept responsibility for violence (e.g., continual blaming of partner, justifying violence, refusing to acknowledge that violence is a problem in his life).

In the case of clients who commit multiple reoffenses or have become violent towards group members, counselors should be very cautious about referring the case to another program or attempting a different treatment modality, because of the risk the client poses to others. For criminal-justice clients, multiple reoffenses may result in a probation revocation hearing and possible incarceration. In non-criminal-justice cases, the victim may be encouraged to call the police and a local battered women's shelter in order to take steps to protect herself and her children. However, here again, there is no guarantee that she will follow up with these referrals. When victims are unable to mobilize their resources to protect themselves, therapists consider involuntary hospitalization of batterers. In extreme cases, victims may be hospitalized or reported to adult protective services if their psychological condition warrants such action. These options are discussed more thoroughly in Chapter Seven, on crisis intervention. In general, frequent reoffenses in and of themselves are not sufficient reason to refer to alternative treatment options unless the alternative program is structured to contain the tendency to act out, such as an inpatient facility.

Likewise, referring clients to another treatment program is not appropriate when they lack internal motivation for change as evidenced by missing sessions, continuing to externalize blame and justify their violence, refusing to acknowledge that violence is a problem at all, or acting intimidating towards others. These individuals are considered at higher risk for violence and are not likely to benefit from counseling. It is not unusual for some batterers to continue resisting change because of a negative relationship that develops between the counselor(s) and the client. Many batterers are extremely sensitive to authority figures, particularly if they grew up with a violent or domineering parent. If this is the case, it would be preferable for counselors to attempt to work out this problem before referring to another provider that could experience a similar interaction with the client. Sometimes, scheduling a number of individual sessions with a client where a negative relationship has developed can help to work through the difficulty without the necessity of a referral.

There are a number of situations when a counselor may consider an alternative referral. Some clients may feel more comfortable in an educational group rather than one that is psychotherapeutic in nature. The boundaries of the educational model may provide the client with the needed structure to contain his intense emotional state. On the other hand, the extremely structured nature of the educational model may, for some clients, be too restrictive and not allow them the opportunity to talk about their experiences. Some clients may do better in group than individual counseling and vice versa. Introverted clients or those lacking in social skills may find the group process too overwhelming. These individuals may also find one-on-one counseling to be equally overwhelming. Educational programs can be very effective for men who have difficulty handling the open process of group or individual counseling.

One specific issue that frequently arises with male batterers is the need to refer for alcohol or drug treatment. The exact relationship between substance abuse and violence has yet to be clearly defined. Suffice it to say that both issues need to be addressed, preferably at the same time. However, if a choice of treatment priorities must be made, I would recommend the substance abuse problem, particularly if the treatment is conducted on an inpatient basis. Outpatient chemical dependency treatment can and should usually be conducted in concert with outpatient violence treatment. Even though many men will be able to abstain from chemical use twenty-four hours before sessions, if an abuse or dependency problem exists they will be unable to utilize the cognitive or behavior interventions between sessions. Therefore clients who are abusing or who are dependent on chemicals need to abstain from use and participate in an alcohol or drug rehabilitation program in order for the Learning to Live without Violence Program (or any violence intervention program, for that matter) to be effective.

SUCCESSFUL COMPLETION OF TREATMENT

The primary goal of treatment is to help men learn alternatives to using violent behaviors to cope with life's problems. Yet, how long should this treatment last? How do we know when we have achieved the goal of stopping the violence? These are difficult questions to answer. We know that many men stop their violence for fear of being arrested or going to jail for violating their probation. If a man has a cycle of violence that lasts six months or a year, how do we know after a twelve-week program that change has occurred and that the violence will not resurface three or six months later? Furthermore, how do we know that after a man successfully completes the terms of his probation he won't become violent again?

Learning to Live without Violence was originally designed as a twelve-week program (one chapter per week). As we revised the book, we changed the chapter titles (from session one, session two, etc., to simply chapter numbers) so that it can also be utilized in six-month (one chapter every other week), twelve-month (one chapter per month), or twenty-four-month programs (refer back to chapters addressed in first three or six months of treatment).

It is unrealistic to believe that a twelve-week education or therapy program will be sufficient intervention to bring about a change in all men who have an established pattern of violence. For those individuals who have only acted violently once or twice and genuinely feel remorse for their actions, a short-term program may be most effective.

However, the majority of batterers referred for counseling have a long history of violent behavior that is well entrenched in their repertoire of responses to stress, conflict, and emotional strife. Therefore, for a large segment of the population of male batterers, longer-term interventions will be necessary to assure recovery.

In order to assess for success of treatment, regular follow-up with the client's partner, while he is in treatment, should be a requirement for acceptance in the counseling program. Periodic couples and family assessment sessions (to be discussed in a later chapter) can also help to determine the degree of change with a particular client. Consultation with other professionals working with a client, such as alcohol and drug counselors or individual or couples counselors, can help assess the progress in treatment.

Unfortunately, no psychometric tool has been developed that assesses a person's risk for future violence. Therefore the counselor must rely on partner reports and on self- and peer-evaluations. These can be therapeutically valuable as well as assist in treatment-planning decisions.

At some point in the process, the client will want to stop or ask if he is ready, or the counselor will want to address the issue of termination with the client; or the probation officer is going to call and ask if treatment has been successful. What should the counselor do? Clients, victims, and law-enforcement personnel need to be told that there are no guarantees that the batterer will stop his violence. There is considerably less risk while a man participates in counseling and a somewhat greater risk subsequent to termination. Counselors can only make an educated guess, in conjunction with other professionals involved with the case, to decide when it is safe to discharge a particular client from counseling. Research in the prediction of violent behavior indicates that mental health professionals are as often right as they are wrong in their predictions. It is probably more clear when not to release a client from counseling than when to terminate. There is no extensive network of self-help meetings like AA or NA that meet seven days a week, twenty-four hours a day, for batterers when even they feel the need for support. Though many men develop and maintain friendships through their programs, these contacts may have minimal use in the middle of the night or when needed in another location.

My experience has indicated that for the majority of the male batterers I have treated, the process was a long-term endeavor; I do not encourage even broaching the idea of a decision to stop until two years have passed. Even at that time, counselors may offer a statement of "no guarantees," and encourage the client and his partner to resume counseling should their relationship begin to deteriorate. You may also want to point out certain behaviors that are indicative that this deterioration process may be occurring, such as frequent or explosive arguments, emotional distancing, nonproductive communication, avoiding contact with each other, increased alcohol or drug use, or psychological violence patterns. Programs may include monthly or quarterly couples assessment sessions subsequent to termination for a number of years, in order to evaluate long-term success and afford the opportunity for the counselor to identify and intervene in problems before they reach a crisis level.

REFERENCES

Goodman, G.S. and Rosenberg, M.S. (1987). *The child witness to family violence: Clinical and legal considerations.* In: D. J. Sonkin (ed.), *Domestic violence on trial: Psychological and legal dimensions of family violence.* New York: Springer Publications.

Hotaling, G.T. and Sugerman, D.B. (1986). An analysis of risk markers in husband to wife violence: The current state of knowledge. *Violence and Victims,* 1 (2), 101-124.

Rosenberg, M.S. (1987). Children of battered women: The effects of witnessing violence on their social problem-solving abilities. *Behavior Therapist,* v10 (4), 85-89.

CHAPTER SEVEN

Crises and Dangerous Situations

Because all domestic violence situations are potentially lethal, counselors must be aware of the legal and ethical situations they may confront in treating this client population (Sonkin, 1986). The four areas
most commonly encountered are: 1) escalating violence toward the
partner or others, 2) depression and suicidal behavior, 3) child abuse
and neglect, and 4) separation and divorce.

DANGER TO OTHERS

The 1976 California Supreme Court decision, *Tarasoff* v. *Regents of
the University of California*, asserted that therapists, because of the
special relationship they have with clients, have a "duty to take reasonable care to protect the intended victim." The case involved a man
who was interested in pursuing a dating relationship with a woman
friend. When he discovered that she was not interested in an ongoing relationship with him, he sought psychological help. To his psychiatrist, he made a specific threat to harm the woman. Although
the psychiatrist notified the police, the court found that he also had a
duty to warn the victim of the patient's threat. This well-known case
established a therapist's "duty to warn" potential victims of violence

threatened by their patients. The court indicated that the reasonable care exercised by the professional could consist of other actions to protect the victim, such as involuntary hospitalization of the patient, but that directly warning the intended victim of the threat is the most effective method to fulfill this duty. Since this opinion, many states have specifically legislated guidelines for therapists in dealing with patients who present a danger to others.

In 1983, another court ruling (*Jablonski by Pahls* v. *United States*) widened the Tarasoff duty to include protecting intended victims of violence even when no specific threat was made. In this case, a psychiatric patient with a serious history of violence towards women killed his wife, even though he did not make any specific threats to her. The court ruled that the psychiatrist should have known that, because of the patient's history of violence, he was likely to commit lethal violence towards his wife, and therefore reasoned that the psychiatrist had a duty to protect her by informing her of the danger her husband posed to her.

Again in 1983, another case broadened the therapist's duty to protect by including *unintended* victims of violence (*Hedlund* v. *Superior Court of Orange County*). In this case, a client made a specific threat to the therapists to harm his wife, which was not communicated to the wife. The client subsequently shot the victim while she and her three-year-old child were in the car. Prior to the shooting, the women threw herself over the child to protect him. The child was not physically injured. The mother had her leg shot off by the shotgun fire. The mother sued the therapists for not warning her of the threats to her, nor of the danger to her child. The court ruled in favor of the mother and child, stating that the therapist had a duty not only to warn the mother of the threat against herself but also to warn her of the danger to her child, since the child was likely to be in close proximity to the mother when the offender would carry out his threat. The court also noted that this did not mean that the therapist must warn unidentifiable bystanders, but that common sense should dictate that certain identifiable persons in close proximity to the victim could also suffer harm and should be warned. This could be taken to include children, roommates, and other family members whom the offender had previously threatened or actually assaulted, or those in close proximity to the potential victim.

It is interesting to note that all three cases involved marital or dating (in the Tarasoff case) violence. These cases, and the statistic that domestic homicide is the largest cause of death of women in the United States, indicate that domestic violence, when left unaddressed, will often escalate to the death of the woman, man, or unintended victims such as children. For this reason, therapists who treat male batterers need to be familiar with the standards of practice and laws and regulations concerning danger, and the duty to protect family members, friends, and other identifiable potential victims.

With the courts' tendency to considerably broaden the duty to protect identifiable victims of violence, mental health professionals in California began to feel uncomfortable with the idea of having to predict violent behavior (Sonkin and Ellison, 1986). Research in the area of violence prediction indicated that therapists were as often wrong as they were right in predicting violent behavior. Therefore, it was argued, placing the burden of making such predictions on the therapist was unfair and unreasonable. Yet therapists indicated that under certain circumstances it would be reasonable to expect a professional to take reasonable care to protect an identifiable victim of threatened violence. For example, research does indicate that individuals who make verbal threats of violence are likely to act on those threats. In 1986, Section 43.92 of the California Civil Code was enacted through legislation. This law indicates that there would be no monetary liability on the part of the therapist in a case where a client makes a specific threat of violence towards an identifiable victim, and the therapist makes a reasonable effort to communicate the threat to the victim and notifies the local law-enforcement agency. This section of the code does not completely overrule Tarasoff; it simply provides a practitioner with a path for immunity. Therefore a practitioner could exercise his or her Tarasoff duty by acting in other ways to protect intended victims of violence (e.g., involuntary hospitalization of the client), yet not be immune from liability.

Because of the high potential lethality in domestic violence cases, it is imperative that the counselor assess for current violence potential throughout the treatment process (Sonkin, 1987). Chapter Four provides guidelines for conducting these evaluations. The following section reviews some of the most important factors to keep in mind when assessing for danger. Keep in mind that, to date, no formula exists that will accurately predict who and who will not continue their violent behavior.

LETHALITY ASSESSMENT FACTORS

- Frequency of physical violence

- Frequency of sexual violence

- Severity of violence (first incident, most frightening, more life-threatening, typical)

- Threats to kill (self, others, partner)

- Frequency of intoxication

- Frequency of alcohol use

- Frequency of drug use

- Proximity of victim and offender

- Psychiatric diagnosis/history

- Client's prior criminal history/activity

- Client's history of violence towards others in family

- Client's history of violence towards others outside of family

- Victim's involvement with others

- Client's attitudes towards violence

Because of the complexity of both the individual and marital dynamics of family violence, decisions regarding lethality should be made by a team of professionals responsible for the monitoring and treatment of both the victim and abuser, if at all possible.

In order to help the clinician take into account all the subtle nuances necessary to make a more accurate determination of potential lethality, the author has developed Lethality Assessment, a comprehensive checklist based on clinical experience and empirical data.

In domestic violence cases the threat of harm is always present, and more so when the offender has a serious psychiatric impairment that interferes with his ability to control his impulses or make use of the therapeutic or educational interventions. Hopefully, the high-risk cases will be identified at an early step in the assessment process. Nevertheless, there will be some men who appear to be a good candidate but later on begin to deteriorate. Therefore, programs should have guidelines in place for handling cases where a client's dangerousness becomes an imminent concern. Counselors should always consult with other professionals before acting to protect the victim from the perpetrator. In this way crisis situations are communicated and jointly considered so that critical decisions are never made by one person.

DEPRESSION AND SUICIDE

As discussed earlier, many male batterers are extremely emotionally dependent on their partner. It is not uncommon for men to experience severe depression as a result of a separation, divorce, or the discovery that their partner is dating another man. Therefore the risk for suicide and suicide/homicide increases during these times. When separation occurs, some men may develop symptoms of severe depression which may include oversleeping or difficulty falling asleep, overeating or lack of appetite, agitation, irritability, difficulty concentrating, low energy, feelings of hopelessness about the current situation or the future, or thoughts of suicide. Extreme anxiety can also accompany depression. Individuals who are depressed usually manifest problems in several areas of life: personal, interpersonal, and occupational. Many male batterers have an extensive family history of mood disorders and therefore may be genetically predisposed to depression. Treatment by medication can take the edge off the depression so that the client is less at risk for suicide or other self-destructive behaviors, and is able to more quickly incorporate the treatment interventions.

Although there is still a stigma attached to seeing a psychiatrist and taking psychotropic medication, many more clients today are open to this alternative because of all the news coverage on medication's potentially beneficial effects. With the proper education on its effects, and with encouragement and support, a counselor can gain a client's cooperation in at least seeing his primary physician or a psychiatrist for a second opinion as to whether or not medication is warranted.

All therapists should already have in place a protocol for handling suicidal clients. As a rule, if suicidal ideation is present, counselors should always receive consultation from other professionals. Other management techniques could also include:

- A no-suicide contract (where the client agrees to meet or speak with the counselor before acting on suicidal impulses)

- Twenty-four-hour watches with family and friends

- An increase in the number of counseling sessions each week

- Daily phone contact with counselor

- The consideration of voluntary hospitalization

In all states, counselors are permitted to violate confidentiality when a client's life is in danger, in order to initiate an involuntary hospitalization. In general, interventions should begin with the least invasive before progressing to the most, unless the client's life is imminently in danger.

Not all batterers who threaten suicide are doing so because of depression. Such threats may be used, like other prior threats, to control or manipulate you or their partner. Therefore, counselors must evaluate the purpose and meaning of the suicide threats. The counselor should note that even if a threat has been assessed as a manipulation or control device, it doesn't mean that the client will not attempt to act on such threats. Therefore, all threats must be taken seriously, by thoroughly documenting the client's statements and the counselor's interventions. Counselors should consult with, and document conversations with, other professionals.

REPORTING CHILD ABUSE AND NEGLECT

Child abuse is particularly prevalent in families where there is spousal violence, making it even more likely that a counselor in a batterer's case may be called upon for such a report (Sonkin and Liebert, in press). A victim of spousal violence may displace her rage at her partner toward the children. Similarly, the spouse-abuser may also be physically, sexually, or psychologically abusing the children. Additionally, exposing a child to spousal abuse is one form of psychological child maltreatment — terrorizing. Psychologist Mindy Rosenberg (1987) indicates that the vast majority of children in violent homes actually hear the violence between their parents. In addition to witnessing violence or being victims of displaced anger or outright abuse, children often try to physically intervene in their parents' violence, mediate their parents' conflict, or get in the way of flying fists or objects.

All states have mandatory reporting laws for child abuse and neglect that require mental health professionals, as well as other specified mandated reporters, to immediately report child physical and sexual abuse and neglect, followed by a written report within a specified period of time. States vary as to what constitutes the minimum standard therapists need for reporting child abuse. For example, California law uses the term *reasonable suspicion,* which means that a mandated reporter only has to reasonably suspect child abuse whether or not they have direct contact with the alleged victim, whereas other states require the therapist to have seen the alleged victim. Additionally, not all states require the reporting of psychological abuse. For example, in California, therapists are not required to report psychological maltreatment unless it is likely to cause great physical or psychological harm.

Numerous studies have indicated that a large number of clinicians inconsistently comply with legal mandates to report abuse. Although it has been speculated that underreporting results from the responsibility being subordinated to the clinicians' policing function and concern for the patient's welfare, others believe that underreporting, in part, stems from differences in the interpretation of the child-abuse laws.

The decision to report or not report is complex where the interests of the individual, the family, the profession, and the community potentially come into conflict. Although most would agree that child abuse is appalling, there are many disagreements as to what actions should be taken to protect children who have been victimized and are at risk for further abuse. The fact that many therapists do not report abuse, in spite of the potential legal and ethical consequences, is evidence that legislation is not a panacea for this complex social phenomenon. In exploring the decision-making process, researchers have determined that a variety of factors influence a therapist's decision. These factors include:

- Responsibility for the abuse

- History of abuse

- Severity of abuse

- Recantation

- Perception of the therapist's role

- Type of abuse

- Socioeconomic status of patient

- License of professional

- Years of practice of therapist

- Clinician's expectation of what effect report would have on individual or family

- The perpetrator's admission or denial of abuse

- Sex of therapist and alleged perpetrator

- Age of child

- Behavior of alleged victim

- Therapist's history of reporting

- Perpetrator's relationship to child

- Therapist's knowledge of law — clarity of legal requirements

In their review of the reporting literature, psychologists Cheryl Brosig and Seth Kalichman (1992) propose a three-tiered approach to decision-making with regard to reporting child abuse: legal factors, clinician characteristics, and situational factors. All three appear to synergistically interact to influence whether or not a clinician chooses to report. Legal factors include the clinician's knowledge of the child abuse laws, the wording of the law itself, and the legal requirements of the law. The clinician characteristics which they suggest relate to child abuse reporting are: the therapist's years of experience, training and attitudes, and experience in making child abuse reports. Lastly, they describe a number of situational factors that also influence a clinician's decision: victim attributes (such as sex, age, and race), types of perpetrated abuse, severity of perpetrated abuse, recentness of abuse, and availability of evidence.

Many clinicians are concerned with the current degree of legislating human behavior, the laws on child abuse and duty to protect being only two examples of this. They maintain that confidentiality is the cornerstone of the therapeutic relationship and that legislating a breach of confidentiality undermines the therapist's ability to do his or her job. The research on the impact of the client-therapist relationship after a child-abuse report indicates that there is either no change or a change for the positive. I would argue that trust, not confidentiality, is the cornerstone of our profession, and that clients trust that we will act in ways that have their best interest in mind — even if the immediate consequences of their actions may cause them pain or discomfort. Certainly the discomfort and embarrassment of the child social services investigation pales in comparison to unnecessary trauma to a child, or criminal charges and a trial resulting from the serious injury or death of a child.

One of the most difficult areas for clinicians is the amount of clinical data or "evidence" necessary to meet the threshold level of reasonable suspicion. Increased evidence results in a greater degree of certainty, which results in a greater probability of reporting. Many reports are not ultimately made because clinicians either do not have enough evidence to support a reasonable suspicion or do not know the "reasonable suspicion" standard for their community. The term *evidence* here refers to the physical and psychological indicators of child abuse, as opposed to the evidence that is used in criminal proceedings to prove guilt beyond a reasonable doubt to a "trier of fact."

Given this information, what can clinicians do to better respond to cases of child maltreatment? Although in many states the law requires a therapist to immediately call social services and follow up with a written report within thirty-six hours once the threshold standard has been met, consultation with colleagues is an important component in assisting the clinician in deciding whether or not to report. In fact, consultation has been found to be positively correlated with reporting of child abuse. Yet this may not always be possible. In those situations when an immediate decision must be made and consultation is not available, a clinician may tell an on-call intake worker at the appropriate agency the relevant facts of the case without initially revealing names of the parties. The intake worker may either ask the right questions that will help the clinician decide the best course of action or will state whether, given the facts described, the reporting threshold has been met or not.

Similarly, it is important for mental health professionals to meet with law enforcement and child protective service personnel in their community to discuss interpretations of the current statutes as well as policies and procedures for reporting and follow-up of cases. Otherwise, clinicians are frequently unaware of the outcome of their reports to child social services. Building a relationship with these professionals tends to enrich the clinical community as well as social service personnel.

Continuing education in the identification and treatment of child abuse will not only increase the clinician's ability to recognize the threshold standard, which assists in more accurate reporting, but will also help them find more effective methods of treating families experiencing this problem. The literature in this field is rapidly expanding to such an extent that even the most experienced clinician needs to take the time to review the latest advances in treatment and research findings. Unfortunately, it is often all too easy for a seasoned clinician to get into a rut by continuing to rely on old research data and treatment methodologies, compromising optimal treatment planning for clients.

Lastly, in order to minimize the trauma experienced by the family as a result of a child-abuse report, many specialists suggest that the clinician make the report (i.e., call social services) while the client(s) are in the office, or ask the client(s) to make the call from the office (the latter being most effective when the treatment is with the perpetrator). A therapist may also attend meetings with police or social services as a support to their client(s) should their presence be desired and appropriate. In general, it is important to recognize that the consequences of the report can be experienced as quite devastating to the client(s) and that the therapist should be available for continued support and assistance during the investigation and evaluation processes.

Feelings of betrayal are likely to be experienced by the patient and/or family members towards the therapist for initiating a report to social services. Therefore, the therapist needs to be prepared for handling a great deal of negative affect when providing appropriate boundaries with the goal of positive resolution in mind. Even so, many clients may not be able to overcome these deep feelings of resentment and lack of trust in the clinician. When this occurs, the therapist needs to seek consultation to evaluate if a referral is appropriate and, if so, to participate in an orderly transition.

SEPARATION AND DIVORCE

When a woman leaves her abuser, the risk for escalated violence may increase, particularly if she is already dating other men. Because many male batterers may be suffering from a disorder of attachment (Dutton, et al., 1994), high levels of anxiety, as well as other dysphoric mood states such as a major depression, may develop when they are involved in intimate relationships. Getting the partner to return is one way of managing this anxiety and is an attempt to dissipate these strong emotions. When reconciliation is not an option for a man, the threat of lethal violence in the form of suicide or homicide, or both, becomes a realistic possibility, particularly for men prone to depression or those very emotionally dependent on their partner.

During a separation or divorce, counselors are encouraged to treat the situation as they would any other crisis where there exists a danger to self or others. Referrals for medication and voluntary or involuntary hospitalization are viable alternatives when a man is unable to control his impulses or assure the therapist that he will not act in self- or other destructive ways. Even for those men who are not at high risk for violence, a divorce or separation represents a time of considerable stress; therefore, the client may need extra support. This may take the form of increasing the frequency of sessions and contact with family and other support systems in order to give him the opportunity to talk out his feelings about the separation or divorce, rather than act out his feelings.

Cognitive therapy has been found to be very effective in the treatment of mood disorders, as well as some personality disorders. Dysfunctional thoughts can contribute to feelings of depression, worthlessness, and hopelessness. Such cognitions and affect are expressed via behaviors. The premise of cognitive theory, although recognizing the synergistic relationship between behavior, cognitions, and affect, states that the best intervention method in changing psychological problems is through altering the cognitions rather than focusing on the emotions. Therefore, interventions that challenge negative or dysfunctional thoughts will alleviate depressive symptomology. Incorporating behavioral interventions, such as those suggested in *Learning to Live without Violence,* gives the man concrete tools to change maladaptive behavioral responses to depression and anxiety. The main focus of cognitive and behavioral interventions is changing dysfunctional thought processes which ultimately contribute to the maladaptive behaviors that all reinforce anxiety and depression.

PROTECT YOURSELF!

Your status and skills as a professional may not be sufficient to protect you if a client threatens you or perceives you as an obstacle to getting away with committing a crime against others. Do not assume that you can talk someone out of harming you or that you can physically protect yourself. There have been numerous cases across the country of batterers attacking or killing their therapists. Programs should have in place plans for emergencies such as these. Office and home alarm systems, video monitoring systems, locked facilities, outdoor lighting, security guards, self-defense education, and preexisting arrangements with local law enforcement agencies can all serve to increase security when treating this client population. Informing clients of these procedures can also help avert a crisis when clients understand that security measures are in place for both your and their protection. Lastly, stay alert and take measures to protect yourself in, as well as outside of, your office as a matter of routine.

REFERENCES

Brosig, Cheryl L. and Kalichman, Seth C. (1992). Clinicians' reporting of suspected child abuse: A review of the empirical literature. *Clinical Psychology Review*, 12 (n2), 155-168.

Dutton, D.G.; Saunders, K.; Starzomski, A.; and Batholomew, K. (1994). Intimacy-anger and insecure attachment as precursors of abuse in intimate relationships. *Journal of Applied Social Psychology*, 24 (15), 1367-1386.

Rosenberg, M.S. (1987). Children of battered women: The effects of witnessing violence on their social problem-solving abilities. *Behavior Therapist*, v10 (4), 85-89.

Sonkin, Daniel Jay (1986). Clairvoyant vs. common sense: Therapist's duty to warn and protect. *Violence and Victims*, 1 (1).

Sonkin, D.J. (1987). The assessment of court-mandated male batterers. In: D.J. Sonkin (ed.), *Domestic violence on trial: Psychological and legal dimensions of family violence.* New York: Springer Publications.

Sonkin, Daniel Jay and Ellison, Jean (1986). The therapist's duty to protect victims of domestic violence: Where we have been and where we are going. *Violence and Victims*, 1 (3).

Sonkin, Daniel and Liebert, Douglas (in press). Legal and ethical issues in the treatment of multiple victimization of children. In: B. Rossman, M. Rosenberg and R. Geffner (eds.), *Multiple victimization of children: conceptual, developmental, research and treatment issues.* New York: Hawarth Press.

CHAPTER EIGHT

Interventions with Couples

Eighteen years ago, when the notion of counseling male batterers was just beginning to become accepted, the idea of counseling couples was not encouraged; in fact, couples or family therapy was touted as being ineffective for this purpose and promoting the belief that women were the cause of men's violence. It was postulated by advocates for victims of domestic violence that focusing on the interaction between the man and woman, otherwise known as the *systems approach*, would give a subtle or not-so-subtle message that the woman was partly responsible for his violent behavior (Bograd, 1984). The distrust of the mental health profession came from the belief that women historically had been blamed for men's problems as well as their own and that couples counseling would only reinforce that erroneous belief. What wasn't considered at the time was that couples counseling could be conducted in such a way as to place responsibility for violence clearly in the hands of the man. Nevertheless, I for one was also guilty of promulgating this notion, even in the face of programs, which I describe below, that were having apparent success through this approach. Like many others, I got caught up in the collective belief that any interpretation of the problem was invalid other than the ideology that prevailed within the movement against domestic violence. You could say I was prejudiced against other forms of intervention because of naiveté and ignorance.

Since that time, the research has not indicated one way or the other that couples counseling with domestic violence clients is as effective — or more or less effective — than separate, same-sex group counseling of victims and offenders. However, through the intervening years, numerous programs and individuals have tried to promote their innovative approaches, receiving strong disapproval from the mainstream advocates against domestic violence. Although I would still agree today — if given a choice, I would conduct perpetrator groups rather than couples intervention for domestic violence cases — I am less dogmatic now. I believe there is a place for couples and family therapy either as the primary intervention or as an adjunct to other approaches, such as separate group or individual counseling of the victim and perpetrator.

DIFFERENT APPROACHES TO COUPLES COUNSELING

There is no one approach to couples counseling — in fact, the term itself is misleading in that orientations to couples therapy vary as much as different types of restaurants. As in approaches to individual counseling, couples therapists vary in their concepts of what helps individuals and couples change and what makes for a successful relationship. Many theorists have based their interventions not so much on research data as on what has worked and makes sense to them, both professionally and personally. One obvious problem with this approach is that not everyone is going to have similar personal philosophies about what constitutes the healthy relationship. Additionally, much of what happens in therapy is dependent on the personalities of the therapist and the client(s) and therefore is unmeasurable or difficult to replicate by other therapists. One can learn theory and technique, but one cannot necessarily transform one's personality. Therefore, the orientation and success one has with couples therapy depend not only on technique and theory but also largely on the personal qualities and belief system of the therapist. The latter gives one considerable leeway in applying a particular theory of intervention with differing couples.

There are many different couples theories. For example, there are those that focus on the individuals and what they bring into the marriage (e.g., object relations couple therapy — Scharff and Scharff, 1991). There are those that focus on the interaction between the individuals (e.g., systems theory — Beavers and Hampton, 1993), and those that focus on how the cultural milieu affects family functioning (e.g., narrative family therapy — Epston, 1994). Individuals who mistake couples therapy as focusing only on the system of interaction between couples may have concluded that approaching domestic violence treatment from this orientation blames the woman for the man's violence. But in fact, one can work with couples without giving the message that the woman is responsible for the man's violence.

Couples therapy that focuses on the individual, such as with the object relations or other developmental theories (Horowitz, Rosenberg, and Bartholomew, 1993), views each member of the couple as bringing into the relationship certain beliefs, feelings, and behavior patterns that have stemmed from early childhood experiences with their parents or parental figures. These childhood experiences help to form core beliefs as to the safety, predictability, and nurturance of persons with whom they are intimate. When childhood experiences include rejection, neglect, or abandonment, an individual is likely to develop a schema for relationships that include these expectations. From this perspective, it would be easy to see how a batterer may perceive and react to certain behaviors by his partner as being rejection, when in fact they are not meant in that way. His partner, on the other hand, may feel extremely frustrated at not being understood. It could be argued that learning to accurately perceive her intentions and not color his perceptions by his prior experiences is as important to the attainment of self-control as is developing specific skills in anger management. Similarly, for the women who was abused as a child, it would be important for her to understand how those experiences affect her perception of her partner and herself — a perception that may only serve to keep her in a relationship where she may not be receiving the love and affection she deserves. This is a superficial example of how understanding internal representations of intimate relationships may affect couples and could be effectively addressed in marital therapy.

Couples counselors utilizing a systems approach to understanding change are not as interested in the etiology of the violence as they are in breaking the cycle of behaviors that contribute to the violence. As mentioned earlier, the systems therapist views the individual as a part, not the whole. The individual is part of a family, a community, a city and country, and so on. Individuals do not solely act alone, but in response to others around them. Systems theory plays down the significance of how individual psychopathology causes certain problems, but rather focuses on how individuals behave and respond to their social contexts. This aspect of systems theory is what makes many domestic violence advocates view this approach as victim-blaming. However, systems theorists strongly argue that their goal is to empower individuals, not contribute to more blaming — a pattern all too common in intimate relationships.

The goal of the systems-oriented couples therapist is to make what are called *second-order changes* (Lane and Russell, 1989). A first-order change is a change in behavior — for example, the man taking time-outs when he is angry or the woman not stopping the man from taking a time-out during an argument. But individuals can make changes in their behavior without making concurrent changes in the relationship dynamic. In other words, there can still exist a dynamic whereby the man and woman do not experience equality by either sharing control or at least taking turns at being in control. Instead, the individuals may have changed specific behaviors, such as by taking a time-out, but the dynamic of victim and victimizer still remains. For a second-order change to occur, both members of the couple must change how they view power and control, communication, and the meaning of intimacy. It is clear from this perspective that couples therapy from a systems orientation can be effective in stopping violence without blaming the victim.

Couples therapists who work from the cultural perspective, such as the narrative approach to family and marital therapy, view the problem of domestic violence as resulting from cultural messages that promote attitudes and behaviors resulting in domestic violence (Jenkins, 1990). In narrative therapy, the cause of the problem is viewed as being external to individuals, such as culture, which heavily influences the way individuals interact. Thinking in terms of problems as being external to people is difficult for many clients to grasp at first. In this way, the *problem* is viewed as the problem, not the *person* as being the problem. Therefore, the problem itself will begin to shape the individual or the relationship.

Then how does having this perspective help to change problems? First, it is a model of nonpsychopathology and therefore doesn't contribute to feelings of low self-esteem. Once the problem is externalized, then the counselor begins to think in terms of direction — the influence of the problem on the person or relationship and the influence of the person or relationship on the problem. For example, take a batterer who has internalized the social message that a real man should always solve his own difficulties. This message will exacerbate his emotional stress and vulnerability to violence if he is unable to allow himself to reach out for help. When he does become violent, he feels worthless as a man because he was unable to solve the real problem himself. This only strengthens his resolve to work it out himself next time. The narrative therapist looks for exceptions, times when the person or relationship was able to break the pattern of the problem rather than continue it. For example, what about the times when he *did* reach out for help and as a result didn't become violent? What does it say about him that he was able to do that? The therapist will interview the person in order to find out how the client viewed that success. In this way the counselor seeks out counterstories as opposed to problem-saturated stories. Because the narrative approach is as much a cultural critique as it is a cultural perspective, the therapist is able to take a stance against bad ideas promulgated by the culture rather than taking a stance against people. In many ways the cultural approach to couples therapy is very much like the gender-analysis approach to domestic violence.

From this brief discussion, one can see how couples therapy orientations alone can differ, much like the approaches to domestic violence treatment elaborated in an earlier chapter. It is also perhaps easier to see how couples treatment could be utilized as either an adjunct to or a primary form of treatment of domestic violence. Let's explore how this may occur.

ADJUNCTIVE COUPLES TREATMENT: THE ASSESSMENT PROCESS

Couples sessions may be utilized in a variety of ways in the treatment of male batterers. As mentioned earlier, a part of the assessment process may include individual sessions with the woman in order to make an accurate determination of the extent and severity of the violence (Sonkin, 1987). Depending on the level of violence and degree of the man's minimization, denial, and externalization, this session may be conducted with the woman alone or in a couples session. Where there is a high level of violence or a great deal of denial, minimization, and externalization, it may be more appropriate to initially meet with the woman alone so that she doesn't experience a subtle intimidation factor that interferes with the information-gathering process. For those men who are more readily accepting responsibility for their behavior, and where the violence history is not extensive, a couples session can be very therapeutic in that it helps the man not only hear about his violence from his partner, but also how his violence has emotionally affected her. This process can also be helpful for men who are less motivated for treatment, but later on in the counseling process. Most importantly, the woman is always given the choice of whether or not she feels comfortable or safe being interviewed in front of her partner. She is informed, beforehand, that she will be asked during the session to disclose the specifics of the history of violence in their relationship. Most women are relieved to talk about the violence with a professional who will believe her and give her the opportunity to express her feelings about the violence. Some women, even though they are fearful of their partner, may prefer a couples interview so that her partner knows exactly what she has told his counselor. Most women are able to accurately determine what type of interview, individual or couples, is best for their particular situation.

Should the woman agree to meeting with her partner, there are three primary purposes for conducting a couples interview during the assessment process. First, the most important reason is for counselors to procure more accurate information about the types and frequency of the violence over the course of their relationship. The man completes the Violence Inventory during his first appointment. During the couples assessment, the woman is also asked to complete the Violence Inventory. The second purpose of the interview is for women to communicate their feelings about the violence so that men can begin to develop an awareness of how their behavior has affected their partner. The third purpose of the couples interview is to explain to the woman the types of behavioral exercises the man will be required to learn and apply to his relationship. It is important to introduce her to techniques, such as the time-out, so that she is aware that some arguments or discussions may not get resolved while her partner is learning how to control his behavior.

When conducting a couples assessment interview, the counselor must focus on these goals and not get distracted by other couples dynamics and problems. In order for a change to occur in the marital/relationship dynamic, there must first be a sense of safety that feelings and thoughts can be communicated without one person becoming violent. It is perhaps the counselor's tendency to focus on underlying interactive processes, rather than directly intervening in the man's violent behavior, that has led feminists and activists to disapprove of couples therapy as a primary mode of intervention in family violence. The temptation is great during these sessions to begin to intervene on the systems level of interaction. However, counselors are encouraged to keep the couples assessment session as being adjunctive to the batterer's treatment model — focusing on his stopping violent behavior rather than moving to interpret violence as resulting from dysfunctional couples interactions.

During this session, the counselor is likely to hear about violence that the woman has perpetrated toward the man. Research has indicated that when women are violent, it is usually after years of victimization or in an attempt to defend herself or stop his violence. Outside of cases of legitimate self-defense, it is important to communicate to the woman that violence is a destructive means of resolving conflict and that she will need to find other ways of communicating anger and frustration and resolving conflict. Generally, women who have been victimized will suffer from mild to severe trauma symptoms. These symptoms may range from anxiety or depressed mood to more dangerous symptoms of suicidal ideation or violence towards others. As a rule, women should be encouraged to seek their own counseling or support so as to work through these symptoms. In doing so, she will better cope with her situation at home, whether that means developing the strength to leave her partner or learning new communication skills in order to interact better with her partner.

ADJUNCTIVE COUPLES TREATMENT: THE ONGOING ASSESSMENT PROCESS

In addition to the couples assessment interview, periodic couples follow-up sessions may be a valuable adjunct to a batterer's treatment. Every six or eight weeks, counselors leading the group may meet with each man and his partner to assess how well he is utilizing the material presented in the weekly counseling sessions. Counselors are already having weekly phone sessions with the partner to determine if violence has occurred between sessions; therefore, the couples sessions can be utilized to assess treatment progress and identify particular issues the man may need to bring back into the group sessions. In these sessions, both the man and woman may discuss how the man has changed the way he interacts with his partner. Primarily, the counselor is assessing for continuing physical, sexual, and psychological violence. Psychological violence, in particular, is difficult to change and therefore is likely to be discussed in these sessions. The partner may either directly or indirectly discuss her fear by focusing on his behaviors that frighten her. For example:

- "I am still afraid of his anger or saying anything that might get him angry."

or

- "He is still yelling a lot."

- "He wants things to go his way."

- "He doesn't like when I go out with my friends."

- "He is still very jealous."

- "He still gets so angry."

Depending on how much the batterer has changed his violent behavior, these couples follow-up sessions can either continue to be violence-focused, like the couples assessment, or more focused on changing relationship dynamics and communication patterns. A man who continues to pose a real danger to his partner, demonstrated either through violent reoffenses or minimization, denial, and externalization, can benefit from the counseling sessions focusing on his violence and confronting his tendency to play down its significance. Men who have made considerable progress in treatment may view the couples follow-up sessions as a precursor to continued couples counseling, and therefore begin to explore other relationship dynamics that contribute to problems in communication, intimacy, etc. For example, a man in this latter category may discuss with his partner how they frequently interrupt each other when discussing controversial issues such as money or children. The couple may also explore how their respective childhood family experiences have contributed to maladaptive patterns in their relationship, other than violence. In either case, the couples follow-up sessions can range from being exclusively focused on the man's violent behavior to the more subtle couples dynamics that may occur in the relationship regardless of the violence.

COUPLES TREATMENT: AN ADJUNCT TO BATTERER'S TREATMENT

In some cases a referral for couples therapy, as an adjunct, may be necessary to enhance the treatment of the batterer. The primary purpose of these referrals may be to help couples manage a continuing crisis, better incorporate the changes the batterer is making in his behavior, and address couples issues that are not being addressed in the periodic couples follow-up sessions.

Counselors to whom you refer these couples should be very familiar with your treatment approach to domestic violence. Most importantly, it is crucial that the client not receive mixed messages regarding responsibility for violence. For example, our program would tell him that no matter what his partner says or does, there is no justification for violence. It would be important that he not receive a message from his couples therapist that his partner plays into the process of escalation and therefore contributes to his violence. Of course, this is a theory that some may use in their treatment of couples, but it is not one that we want conveyed to our clients. Therefore, batterers programs that do use adjunctive couples treatment need to be aware that opposing messages may get conveyed to clients. Close coordination between therapists is necessary to avoid this problem.

Couples therapy as an adjunct can definitely enhance the group batterers treatment (and perhaps speed it along) for several reasons. First, the additional therapy appointment each week gives the man a continuing opportunity to identify and communicate his feelings with the help of a third party. Second, for some men (and women too), the need to talk about the marital problems, over and above the violence, may be too great to wait every six weeks for the couples follow-up sessions. Third, weekly couples counseling can help to manage and prevent crises that the batterers program counselors may not have the staff or time to treat. Lastly, weekly couples counseling can greatly help batterers incorporate the material they are learning in their program into their relationship.

COUPLES TREATMENT: THE PRIMARY MODE OF TREATMENT

Because this book focuses on the use of *Learning to Live without Violence: A Handbook for Men* in groups for male batterers, it is not within its scope to offer a thorough discussion of treating couples experiencing domestic violence. Additionally, as discussed earlier, there are many different ways of working with couples within the context of domestic violence. At the end of this book, there is a list of books and articles that the reader may find helpful in designing interventions specifically for couples. However, I would like to present a brief discussion of factors that I and others have identified as helpful to consider when conducting couples therapy with families experiencing domestic violence.

Female/male co-therapy teams. When I began working with domestic violence in the mid- to late 1970s, I worked with couples with a female co-therapist. We found this helpful for a number of reasons. Because perpetrators and victims of violence are often in extreme crisis and as a result may be vulnerable to wanting an ally or suspicious that others are not likely to support their point of view, either member of the couple may perceive a single therapist as taking sides because of her or his gender. A man may see a male therapist as taking sides with his wife or the wife may see the male therapist as taking sides with her husband. Similarly, the female therapist may also be perceived as being partial towards one member of the couple or the other. A co-therapy team can somewhat defuse this process, since each member of the couple ostensibly has someone to identify with and therefore may believe that the therapist is likely to be "on their side."

Another reason for the female/male co-therapy team approach is to model positive communication, cooperation, and teamwork — qualities necessary for a healthy marriage. Co-therapists may communicate with each other, within the session, about what they are observing in the couple, which helps the couple develop skills in stepping outside their conflict and observing their patterns of interaction. The counselors may also discuss their individual perceptions of the couple. This discussion may include where their perceptions overlap and where they differ. Differences may simply be accepted or resolved in front of the couple, both choices serving as a positive role model for couples.

Another advantage of working with a co-therapist is that domestic violence couples, because of their crises, may present themselves as being overwhelmed by all the issues they need to address. A co-therapist can help prevent a single therapist from similarly becoming overwhelmed by the material and consequently ineffectual with the couple. Furthermore, working with a live supervision team behind a one-way mirror can also help the co-therapy team not only identify patterns within the couple but interaction patterns between the therapists.

Responsibility rather than blame. All couples, at one time or another, in the course of their relationship blame one another during a conflict or disagreement. This pattern is no different in couples experiencing domestic violence. However, this may be more pervasive because of the frequency and severity of the crises experienced. Because of this common dynamic, couples therapists try to help each member of the couple examine how they contribute to the unhappiness of the relationship. For the man, among other things, it is certainly his violent behavior. For the woman it could be alcohol or drug abuse, a critical or judgmental nature, or infidelity. Therefore, the therapists need to find a way of helping both members of the couple look at themselves as needing to change in order for the relationship to improve. One could argue that if he stopped his violence, the relationship would dramatically improve. Yet experience has not shown this to be the case. If the woman doesn't simultaneously work through her anger and fear, then many of the patterns of interaction will continue as if the violence were continuing. This phenomenon may be compared to those alcoholic families where the drinker gets into recovery and yet the partner continues to act like the drinker is still drinking.

The message must be given to both members of the couple that each person is responsible for his or her own behavior. Although couples constantly react and respond to one another in both conscious and unconscious ways, both persons must take responsibility for their own feelings, thoughts, and behavior. Unlike the light switch and the light, which are inextricably linked by wires and dependent on the laws of physics, each person can make choices as to whether, or not, or how, to respond to the other person.

Assessment of violence and other emergencies. Couples counselors are frequently confronted with crises, such as suicidal individuals, and decide to intervene in the crisis before addressing relationship issues. With domestic violence cases runs the high risk of life-threatening violence and homicide. Therefore, the counselors should routinely conduct an initial assessment for severity of violence. Counselors may assess that the risk for lethal violence is too great to work with the couple alone. Collateral referrals to a batterer's and a battered woman's program may be necessary for some couples too entrenched in violence.

Other crisis issues, such as depression and suicide, alcoholism, and drug abuse must also be identified early on in treatment in order to formulate a realistic couples treatment plan. Collateral referrals for psychiatric or drug and alcohol evaluations may be necessary in order to prepare the couple for psychological availability to effective couples therapy. In some cases, couples therapy may need to be put "on hold" until other evaluations are conducted and decisions are made regarding the need for inpatient or outpatient treatment. Should one member of the couple need hospitalization for a psychiatric issue or chemical dependency, couples therapy could be a part of either the inpatient program or the discharge plan. These decisions could be made in conjunction with hospital staff.

Types of interventions. The anger management and couples communication material presented in the *Learning to Live without Violence* workbook has been successfully used with both violent and nonviolent couples. As described earlier, there are many different approaches to working with couples. However, with domestic violence couples, the most common approaches to treatment focus on education and cognitive and behavioral interventions (all similar to those described in *Learning to Live without Violence*). As mentioned before, more systemic (systems-theory) intervention programs focus on interactional dynamics within the relationship, maladaptive perceptions of the pair, and historical antecedents that contribute to violent patterns in the relationship. Many approaches with couples also integrate a social analysis of domestic violence as a part of the education and interventions. Most importantly, the programs described in the literature all tend to clearly focus on the abuse, with one of the most important goals of treatment being to stop recurrent patterns of violent behavior. Even though a particular program might consider that women may directly contribute to the escalation process in the relationship, a theory scorned by feminists and activists, the interventions are nevertheless primarily directed at stopping violent behavior by both members of the couple. As with many other social ills that individuals and groups are attempting to solve, there are many different approaches to intervening with domestic violence couples, reflecting different philosophies as to the cause of the problem.

Evaluation of interventions. Because of the inherent danger in families experiencing domestic violence, counseling programs should be particularly careful to evaluate the effectiveness of their intervention approaches. The few studies that have been conducted at various programs across the country indicate that intervening with perpetrators and victims is effective. What is considered success may differ from program to program. For example, some intervention programs may consider stopping physical and sexual violence as success, as opposed to another program that would include the cessation of psychological violence in the definition of success. For some couples treatment programs, the decision to divorce and go separate ways may be considered a success, whereas another program may consider only those couples who stay together and work out their problems as being successful. No matter what the criteria for success, the question remains: how long do treatment effects last? Typically, evaluations are conducted six or twelve months after termination from treatment. It is unclear if this is a sufficient period of time to determine if violence will resurface within a relationship. Therefore, counselors should be cautious as to claims made about the effectiveness of a particular approach to treating domestic violence.

THE VALUE OF DIFFERENT APPROACHES TO TREATMENT

Although it's considered controversial, and disapproved of by some outspoken individuals and groups, there does exist a place for couples work with families experiencing domestic violence. From couples assessment and follow-up in a batterers treatment program, to adjunctive couples treatment secondary to batterers treatment, to couples treatment as a primary form of intervention, couples interventions can be useful in stopping domestic violence.

It has only been twenty years since the first book on domestic violence appeared in the United States, and therefore we are in the infancy stages of finding enduring solutions to this tragic social problem. The battered women's movement has been the primary force behind most of the advances in both the psychological and social arenas and offers a perspective necessary to solve this problem on a global level. Yet large-scale changes begin with individuals, and individuals are very complex and therefore in need of complex solutions to this problem. The individual, relationship, and social analysis of the problem of family violence each offer a unique perspective to the issue of domestic violence. By incorporating all three, perhaps one could create a comprehensive treatment theory and approach that would supersede any one individually. It appears that a couples theory of intervention may offer an approach that incorporates all three perspectives. Perhaps our worst fears of couples intervention have not been realized.

REFERENCES

Beavers, W. Robert and Hampton, Robert B. (1993). Measuring family competence: The Beavers Systems Model. In: Froma Walsh (ed.), *Normal family processes* (2nd ed.). Guilford family therapy series. New York: Guilford Publications, pp. 73-103.

Bograd, M. (1984). Family systems approaches to wife battering: A feminist critique. *American Journal of Orthopsychiatry*, 54 (4), 558-568.

Epston, D. (1994). Extending the conversation: Letters can be powerful tools for reauthoring lives. *Family Therapy Networker*, Nov./Dec.

Horowitz, L.M.; Rosenberg, S.E.; and Bartholomew, K. (1993). Interpersonal problems, attachment styles and outcome in brief dynamic psychotherapy. *Journal of Consulting and Clinical Psychology*, 61 (4), 549-560.

Jenkins, Alan (1990). *Invitations to responsibility: The therapeutic engagement of men who are violent and abusive.* Adelaide, South Australia: Dulwich Centre Publications.

Lane, G. and Russell, T. (1989). Second-order systemic work with violent couples. In: P.L. Caesar and L.K. Hamberger (eds.), *Treating men who batter: Theory, practice and programs.* New York: Springer Publications.

Scharff, David E. and Scharff, Jill Savege (1991). *Object relations couple therapy.* Northvale, NJ: Jason Aronson, Inc.

Sonkin, D.J. (1987). The assessment of court-mandated male batterers. In: D.J. Sonkin (ed.), *Domestic violence on trial: Psychological and legal dimensions of family violence.* New York: Springer Publications.

CHAPTER NINE

Cross-cultural Issues

Until recently, most of the written material examining the cross-cultural/ethnic issues relating to domestic violence has been found in training manuals and curricula developed by battered women's programs. Mental health professionals have not conducted systematic research or developed clinical interventions specific to populations of color. As a result, many of the programs and interventions developed for male batterers in this country have been conceived from the Eurocentric point of view, not thoroughly taking into account the unique perspective of the man of color. *Learning to Live without Violence* may be criticized in this way as well, even though it was written with the idea of appealing to the broadest cross-section of male batterers. Yet, as was discussed earlier, the population of male batterers is not a homogeneous one — in fact, there is considerable research indicating that there may be many different types of batterers. Although some may argue that male violence against women supersedes culture, researchers are now finding that ethnicity and culture are critically important when considering community response systems and treatment interventions for victims and offenders. Therefore, a consideration of the cross-cultural counseling theories is necessary in order for counselors to begin to integrate ethnicity/culture into violence treatment theory and approaches.

Compared to general domestic violence literature, research and clinical materials on domestic violence in families of color is minuscule. A literature search on this topic with psychological abstracts found over fifteen hundred citations on the topic of domestic violence, whereas there were only fifteen citations on the topic of domestic violence and ethnicity. Most of these articles were published in the last four years; many of them focus on the rates of occurrence, etiology (causes), and suggestions for community and individual interventions.

Studies with Latin (Torres, 1991; Diaz, 1989; Parilla, Bakeman, and Norris, 1994; Rodriguez, 1986; Rouse, 1988), Asian (Ho, 1990; Frye and D'Avanzo, 1994; Song, 1986), Native American (Black Bear, 1988; DeBruyn, Hymbaugh, and Valdez, 1988; Gotowiec and Beiser, 1993-94; Larose, 1989) and African-American (Brice-Baker, 1994; Campbell, Campbell, King, Parker, and Ryan, 1994; Finn, 1986; Hampton, 1987; Lockhart and White, 1989; Lockhart, 1987; Marsh, 1993; Uzzell and Peebles-Wilkins, 1989) families indicate that although rates of occurrence may not differ between people of color and majority culture individuals, women and men of color face unique challenges that must be taken into consideration when formulating treatment, criminal justice, and social service responses.

One difference in particular is the history and continual experience of oppression and racism that people of color encounter on a daily basis. These experiences, together with the belief that the various protective systems set up to provide services (e.g., police, social services, or the courts) will not act in a protective fashion, may serve to ultimately prevent a battered woman from seeking help from others. In addition, discrimination in employment and economic inequality create tremendous barriers for battered women of color to escape their violent partners. Evidence exists that people of color may experience extreme stress in the daily task of navigating between their own and the majority culture (Anderson, 1991; Gaines and Reed, 1995). The results of this stress, added to the reality of experiencing racism, dealing with difficulties inherent in day-to-day living, and being a victim of violence, can tax an individual's coping resources to their maximum abilities (Koss, Goodman, Fitzgerald, Russo, Keita, and Browne, 1994).

There are several problems that arise when addressing the issue of ethnic minorities and domestic violence. First, there exists the danger of overgeneralizing specific ethnic groups by saying all "African-American men do this," or all "Asian-American men do that." Doing so perpetuates stereotypes that contribute to prejudice and racism. Second, when we discuss the history of racial injustice experienced by many people of color in this country, it may begin to sound as though oppression is the reason for domestic violence. Although the effects of racism may play an important role in a man's life, it does not mean that racism is the *only* cause of domestic violence. Saying so only promotes the myth that men of color are dangerous, because all men of color have experienced racism to one degree or another. It is well known that the vast majority of persons belonging to ethnic minorities in the United States are law-abiding citizens. All people of color have to contend with the effects of racism on a daily basis, and yet the majority of these individuals do not beat their wives or commit other crimes. However, one cannot underplay the effects that racism may have on a particular individual. Differences exist between individuals as to how they experience and are affected by various social stressors. As a white male, I may be criticized for attempting to address this issue because, as a member of a majority culture, I benefit from white privilege and therefore know little of what it is like to be a victim of racism. Because I am white, I enjoy the privilege of being a member of a majority culture in many ways. However, because I am also Jewish, I have experienced antisemitism and therefore can also understand, to some degree, the experience of racism from the other side of the fence.

How can we find ways of addressing the unique needs of ethnic minorities seeking services for domestic violence? Perhaps it would be useful to look into the general literature relating to psychotherapy services for minorities.

TREATMENT SERVICES FOR ETHNIC MINORITIES

There have been two decades of research into the adequacy of psychotherapy services for ethnic minorities, and yet many service providers are as perplexed as ever as to how to increase the effectiveness of these services. In the early 1980s, the Special Populations Task Force of the President's Commission on Mental Health indicated that ethnic minorities are underserved or inappropriately served by the mental health system. This fact has only somewhat changed in the past ten years. One study in the Seattle area found that some populations were overrepresented, whereas others were underrepresented. However, regardless of the utilization rates, all ethnic minority clients have a higher dropout rate than whites. Ethnic minorities had a fifty percent dropout rate, as opposed to a thirty percent dropout rate for whites.

How can this problem be explained? Many ethnic minorities either avoid services or drop out because of the lack of bilingual services. In addition, most mental health intervention theories are based on the white majority culture and, therefore, ethnic- or culture-specific behaviors are either framed as pathological or not understood as potentially helpful in solving interpersonal problems. Likewise, in addition to this ignorance, many therapists hold racist attitudes to which clients are acutely sensitive. Most importantly, therapists today — most of whom are still of the majority culture — have difficulty providing culturally responsive forms of interventions. Most majority-culture therapists are not familiar with the cultural backgrounds and lifestyles of the various ethnic minority groups they serve. Consequently, they are unable to devise culturally sensitive forms of treatment. Ethnic minorities often find mental health services strange, foreign, or unhelpful. For example, Latinos value linearity, role-structured rather than egalitarian relationships, and a present-time orientation. African-American cultural traditions include group identification, extended family kinship networks, spirituality, and a flexible concept of time. When the counselor fails to recognize these differences, it becomes an impediment to effective treatment. These traditions, along with the client's reactions to a history of racial oppression, must be understood by counselors in order to truly understand the ethnic minority's experience of life in the majority culture that white therapists take for granted.

The President's Commission recommended that, in the best of all possible worlds, services would be delivered by, or there would always be the option of, professionals who share the same value system, beliefs, and class experience of the client being served. However, this scenario is far from attainable at this time. In order to move toward this possibility, graduate training programs would need to expand their outreach efforts so as to better represent the diversity of ethnic groups in the larger culture.

Similarly, programs also need to better train students on how to address the needs of ethnic minorities by developing sensitivity to other cultures and altering traditional psychotherapy techniques accordingly. However, knowledge is not enough to provide culturally sensitive psychotherapy services, because cultural knowledge and "techniques" can often be applied in inappropriate ways.

Another way of teaching cultural sensitivity is by helping majority-culture therapists to become aware of their own ethnic identity. Also a historical knowledge of minority cultures and the prejudice and racism they have encountered is necessary to understand the cultural context that many clients have to continually struggle with on a daily basis. However, most importantly, new paradigms of cross-cultural counseling need to be developed so that therapists can reformulate how they approach psychotherapy with ethnic minorities.

Stanley Sue, a psychologist at UCLA, describes two basic processes that are important to consider when working with ethnic minorities — credibility and giving (Sue and Nolan, 1987). Obviously these are not the only elements necessary for effective cross-cultural counseling, but they are important and worth considering in working with minority-culture male batterers.

"Credibility" refers to the client's perception of the therapist as an effective and trustworthy helper. Therapeutic success is increased when the client believes in the process, in that the methods being employed are credible. Credibility may be divided into two components: ascribed and achieved status.

Ascribed status is the position or role in which the therapist is placed by the client before the counseling even begins. These elements may include the client's perception of counseling and the counselor's age, sex, race, and experience. Minority clients may enter into counseling with the expectation that the experience is not going to be helpful. They may view therapy as another majority culture institution that is racist and oppressive. This notion may be particularly reinforced if the counselor is white. These factors all contribute to the low ascribed status the mental health profession has with ethnic minorities.

Achieved status refers more directly to the therapist's skills and knowledge. Through the actions of the therapist, clients may come to have faith, trust, confidence, or hope that the outcome will be positive. The achieved status is likely to be directly related to the counselor's experience, but equally important, the increase in status is likely to occur when the therapist intervenes in a culturally consistent manner.

By analyzing the credibility we may begin to understand how we can better respond to the therapeutic needs of minority-culture clients. Credibility helps us to understand why ethnic-minority clients may either underutilize the treatment opportunity or prematurely drop out. When the ascribed status is low, clients are likely to avoid counseling altogether. When the ascribed status is somewhat higher but the achieved status is low, a client may enter therapy but prematurely terminate because the counselor may not be addressing the client's cultural needs. This process does not mean that the therapist should support or match clients' beliefs that are ultimately interfering with problem resolution; however, incongruities in cultural beliefs and therapeutic orientation can lead to decreased achieved status and premature termination of treatment. By focusing on credibility rather than just techniques and information, therapists will use culture-specific techniques when necessary and not use culture-specific approaches for the clients who would not benefit from them.

Clients often wonder how talking about problems can bring about a change in their life situation. "Giving" is the client's perception that something was received from the therapeutic encounter. The client has received a "gift" from the therapist. Typically, therapists attempt to raise the clients' expectation that they will receive something for their efforts. For many clients, this expectation is sufficient to set aside their immediate needs in favor of something they may receive in the future. For ethnic minorities, because of the high dropout rate, it is critically important that counselors not simply raise their client's expectations but help them to feel that they are receiving a direct benefit from the session. Typically, the first few sessions of counseling are focused on the therapist-collected information. For the ethnic minority, where there may be a great deal of skepticism about unfamiliar methods of treatment or institutions that have historically been used to oppress people, it is important to help the client attain some type of meaningful gain right from the onset of counseling. These gifts may include behavioral interventions, providing structure or clarity during a crisis, and normalizing certain thoughts and feelings within a cultural context. In some cases, it may be appropriate to give a client an actual gift, such as a book.

Obviously these are not new ideas, but they can be very helpful in beginning to structure counseling interventions that can provide culturally relevant services to ethnic minorities. Historically, psychology has placed a great deal of emphasis on gaining knowledge of ethnic minorities without much focus on how to apply that knowledge to the actual counseling process. In order to effectively counsel ethnic minorities, we must learn about our own ethnic identity and the culture of others, and at the same time develop new ways of clinically applying that knowledge.

RACISM AND VIOLENCE IN SOCIETY

All ethnic minority groups in the United States have at one time or another been victim to institutionalized oppression by the government — from the Native Americans' Trail of Tears and the slavery of the African-Americans, to the internment of Japanese-Americans during World War II, to recent legislation in California aimed at prohibiting medical, educational, and financial aid to illegal Latin immigrants. The United States was founded on the hope that the country would be a homogeneous group of white, Protestant Europeans. Yet ironically, throughout history other social forces have brought other ethnic groups to this country, making it one of the most heterogeneous populations in the world. Still today, prejudice and racism are rampant across the country, ultimately contributing to the economic and emotional suffering of millions of people.

This history of oppression of others has exacted a high price to the majority culture. Anger, distrust, and bitterness towards whites and the institutions which they represent have contributed to many social ills, such as crime, urban decay, and violence. The Mexican-American child, who is denied adequate education because of the lack of financial resources of the parent, has a greater chance of dropping out of school and stealing the white man's BMW. The learning-disabled African-American child, who was prematurely born because of inadequate medical services to his mother, will ultimately cost all Americans more in taxes if he doesn't receive specialized education and instead is labeled stupid. In addition to the social losses, many individuals experience personal pain resulting from racism, such as not being able to pursue certain friendships because of social pressures against intermingling.

Prejudice is defined as prejudging another or forming an opinion of an individual or group of individuals based on limited information. All of us have prejudices based on the various cultural stereotypes to which we have been exposed during our lifetime. Racism may be defined as prejudice plus power. It is a system of advantage based on race (Tatum, 1992). It is virtually impossible to live in contemporary society and not be exposed to some aspect of personal, cultural, or institutionalized racism. Therefore, all people will internalize, to one degree or another, some negative attitudes or beliefs about people of color. In order to break the cycle of prejudice and racism we all need to take responsibility for reeducating ourselves, identifying negative attitudes, and changing behaviors.

A white therapist may say, "I am not a part of the institutional-ization of racism in the country. I don't have power to promote racist policies. Why would a person of color distrust me?" First of all, psychology for many years contributed to myths and the misunder-standing of minorities by promoting research that promulgated the belief that they were inferior to whites. Second, psychotherapeutic principles were developed on the basis of experience with white, middle-class individuals and therefore reflect that bias. Many ethnic minorities find traditional mental health interventions to be peculiar and in some cases disrespectful of their values and traditions. Lastly, licensed mental health providers do have power to affect people's lives. They have the power to report different forms of abuse, power to hospitalize, power to refuse treatment, power to affect insurance re-imbursement, power to help or not help, to name but a few. When seen from this point of view, the perspective of the ethnic minority, one can understand how historical and contemporary social treat-ment of ethnic minorities can have an effect on an individual's atti-tude towards mental health services.

Although many Americans, both white and ethnic minorities, today suffer economic or emotional problems, the person of color has the added burden of dealing with prejudice and racism on a daily basis. Mothers and fathers, in addition to struggling to survive, need to teach their children the realities of racism in society while not overwhelming them to the point that they give up before they begin. Many people, mostly white, believe that prejudice and racism are not a problem today, many years after the civil rights movement. What has changed somewhat is the blatant racism of the years of slavery. However, this blatant hatred of people of color has in many ways gone underground and therefore has taken on more subtle forms. Centuries of ignorance and hatred are not easily changed overnight. If you are uncertain if this is the reality, just ask a person of color, of any class, if a racism problem in America still exists.

What is the relationship between prejudice, racism, and domes-tic violence? Sociologists are trying to answer this question by exam-ining the effects of racism on the development of children. Studies indicate that overt and subtle forms of racism can exact a high toll on the self-esteem of children. We know that low self-esteem has been correlated with a variety of problems including alcohol and drug abuse and violence. We also know that low self-esteem can interfere with an individual's performance in academic or employment activities. It is well known, too, that poverty also exacerbates whatever psychological problems an individual experiences, in that it compounds the stressors one must overcome in order to succeed. Studies indicate, fairly consistently, that a history of childhood abuse may lead to a problem with violence as an adolescent or adult. Many adults who grew up in violent homes suffer from low self-esteem. Racism in all its overt and subtle manifestations will have some degree of psychological impact on an individual and therefore will only worsen whatever emotional toll is taken on the child who witnesses or is victim of violence during childhood.

CROSS-CULTURAL COUNSELING WITH MALE BATTERERS

First it is important to recognize that, to one degree or another, every person of color entering into a batterer treatment program has experienced prejudice and racism. Do not be afraid of communicating to the client that you recognize the extent to which race and racism may play a significant role in his life and that he doesn't have to protect you from his experiences and feelings about it. This issue may become most critical with the court-mandated client. He may feel that the system has treated him more harshly than his white male counterpart. He may feel that he is being victimized by white culture and the courts. Although there is doubtless some truth to the client's observation, the counselor must combine sensitivity to his feelings with helping him take responsibility for his problem with violence. One of the advantages of group counseling is that clients can see that men of all ethnic backgrounds are experiencing the problem of domestic violence and are being held accountable by the criminal justice system.

Therapists should not assume that social class protects an individual from the effects of societal racism. Just as poverty compounds the psychological effects of racism, middle- and upper-class status can also complicate how one deals with racism. Many middle- and upper-class men of color may feel guilt for "making it" and leaving others behind. He may also use much of his hard-earned money supporting other family members. Many highly educated African-American males confront invisible barriers at work and school. They may be confronted with hostility if they are the first person of color in a particular occupation or status within a company.

If we were to utilize Sue's theory of credibility and giving in understanding the cross-cultural counseling of male batterers, it could help us understand why some men of color may have difficulty with the various treatment programs developed by domestic violence advocates and clinicians.

For the most part, men in general do not hold counseling services in high esteem, therefore the ascribed status will be low. Men of color, for the reasons described earlier, may view counseling in even less favorable ways. This expectation could be somewhat mitigated if the counselor is of the same ethnic group or older in age. But a white counselor will need to pay particular attention to achieved status as a way to facilitate the minority client's connection with the counseling process. Even for the court-mandated client, resistance to change, acting out, or uncooperative behaviors could develop if the counselor is not sensitive to the cultural issues. Additionally, if one of the goals of counseling male batterers is raising self-esteem, then it would follow that addressing cultural contributors to low self-esteem would be important in minimizing the psychological stress that can in turn raise the risk for domestic violence.

Another way for counselors to work towards increasing achieved status is to learn specific cultural characteristics, integrating this knowledge into the counseling approach. Counselors should not be afraid to directly ask clients about their cultural values, but they should not use this technique as a replacement for learning about the specific ethnic groups. For example: with Native Americans, counselors may allow longer silences or pose questions that guide and advance rather than highly directive ones; with African-Americans, counselors might need to recognize the value of extended family kinship and the stressing of nonverbal communication skills; with Asian-Americans, counselors may need to appreciate their strong family values of privacy and nondisclosure, hierarchical family roles, and the connection between emotional and physical problems; with Hispanic Americans, the counselor may need to recognize the strong patriarchal family patterns, incorporation of spiritual practices, and the value of *personalismo* (personal greeting, handshaking, the use of first names and small talk) for developing rapport. It is beyond the scope of this chapter to give the reader a comprehensive understanding of all the cultural values in all the various ethnic groups, so a section on cross-cultural issues is included in the reading list at the end of this book. Certainly, counselors should become familiar with the body of literature on cross-cultural counseling.

If we were to redesign the Learning to Live without Violence Program, or any other approach, for ethnic minority groups we might need to reconceptualize the problem, change the means for problem resolution, and possibly change the goals of treatment. Obviously, the main goal of domestic violence treatment must be the safety of all family members; therefore, the abuser must stop his destructive behavior. If we maintain this goal, we can see how it can become possible to develop another approach to treatment of male batterers. For Native Americans the problem may be conceived as a spiritual illness, and therefore the client may need to visit a medicine person or another spiritual leader in the tribe. One part of the treatment plan may include a "vision quest" or a series of "sweats" or "chants." An Asian-American client's violence may be attributed to an imbalance in energy forces within the boy and therefore he might need to receive herbal or acupuncture treatments. Or, an elder relative may be brought into treatment to help motivate the client to deal with his problem with violence. A Hispanic or African-American man may benefit from family therapy and advocacy services that address important social needs which may be strongly contributing to stress and conflict at home.

Lastly, the best way to develop treatment approaches specific to ethnic populations is to offer counseling services for individual groups led by professionals who identify with the same cultural and class background. Because the vast majority of clinicians who have written about treatment of male batterers are of majority-culture ethnicity, the most commonly used treatment interventions and program philosophies represent a Eurocentric point of view. Though it has been very difficult in the past for a man of color to find a homogeneous group, this is changing today in that more programs are developing services for specific ethnic populations. Volcano Press has received many requests for a translation of *Learning to Live without Violence* into Spanish. At the time of this writing, this project is already underway. As more and more programs offer services specifically for men of color, a culturally relevant treatment paradigm is likely to evolve over time. This was how many of the interventions in *Learning to Live without Violence* were developed. This approach evolved over years of refinement by ethnically heterogeneous groups of men. The structure more or less grew out of the program, rather than being devised and then simply imposed on the men.

REFERENCES

Anderson, Louis P. (1991). Acculturative stress: A theory of relevance to Black Americans. *Clinical Psychology Review*, v11 (n6), 685-702.

Black Bear, Tillie (1988). Native American clients. In: Anne L. Horton and Judith A. Williamson (eds.), *Abuse and religion: When praying isn't enough*. Lexington, MA: Lexington Books/D.C. Heath and Company, pp. 135-136.

Brice-Baker, Janet R. (1994). Domestic violence in African-American and African-Caribbean families. Special Issue: Multicultural views on domestic violence. *Journal of Social Distress & the Homeless*, Jan., v3 (1), 23-38.

Campbell, Doris Williams; Campbell, Jacquelyn; King, Christine; Parker, Barbara; and Ryan, Josephine (1994). The reliability and factor structure of the index of spouse abuse with African-American women. *Violence and Victims*, v9 (3).

DeBruyn, Lemyra M.; Hymbaugh, Karen; and Valdez, Norma (1988). Helping communities address suicide and violence: The Special Initiatives Team of the Indian Health Service. *American Indian & Alaska Native Mental Health Research*, Mar., v1 (3), 56-65.

Diaz, Daniel P. (1989). Hispanic and Anglo marital conflict resolution and marital violence. *Dissertation Abstracts International*, Jan., v49 (7-B), 2850.

Finn, Jerry (1986). The relationship between sex-role attitudes and attitudes supporting marital violence. *Sex Roles*, Mar., v14 (5-6), 235-244.

Frye, Barbara A. and D'Avanzo, Carolyn D. (1994). Cultural themes in family stress and violence among Cambodian refugee women in the inner city. *Advances in Nursing Science*, Mar., v16 (n3), 64-77.

Gaines, S.O. and Reed, E.S. (1995). Prejudice: From Allport to DuBois. *American Psychologist*, 50 (2), 96-103.

Gotowiec, Andrew and Beiser, Morton (1993-94). Aboriginal children's mental health: Unique challenges. *Canada's Mental Health*, Winter, v41 (4), 7-11.

Hampton, Robert L. (1987). *Violence in the black family: Correlates and consequences*. Lexington, MA: Lexington Books/D.C. Heath and Company.

Ho, Christine K. (1990). An analysis of domestic violence in Asian-American communities: A multicultural approach to counseling. Special issue: Diversity and complexity in feminist therapy: I. *Women & Therapy*, v9 (n1-2), 129-150.

Koss, M.; Goodman, L.; Fitzgerald, L.; Russo, N.F.; Keita, G.P.; and Browne, A. (1994). *No safe haven: Male violence against women at home, at work and in the community.* Washington, DC: American Psychological Association.

Larose, François (1989). L'environnement des réserves Indiennes est-il pathogene? Réflexions sur le suicide et l'identification des facteurs de risque en milieu Amerindien Québecois. (Is the environment of Indian reservations...) *Revue Québecoise de Psychologie,* v10 (1), 31-44.

Lockhart, Lettie L. (1987). A reexamination of the effects of race and social class on the incidence of marital violence: A search for reliable differences. *Journal of Marriage & the Family,* Aug., v49 (3), 603-610.

Lockhart, Lettie and White, Barbara W. (1989). Understanding marital violence in the black community. *Journal of Interpersonal Violence,* Dec., v4 (4), 421-436.

Marsh, Clifton E. (1993). Sexual assault and domestic violence in the African-American community. *Western Journal of Black Studies,* Fall, v17 (3), 149-155.

Parilla, Julia L.; Bakeman, Roger; and Norris, Fran H. (1994). Culture and domestic violence: The ecology of abused Latinas. *Violence and Victims,* v9 (3).

Rodriguez, Vivianne (1986). Attitudes towards corporal punishment, social support system, and conflict resolution techniques related to family violence in Puerto Rican families living in the United States. *Dissertation Abstracts International,* Mar., v46 (9-A), 2635.

Rouse, Linda P. (1988). Abuse in dating relationships: A comparison of Blacks, Whites, and Hispanics. *Journal of College Student Development,* Jul., v29 (4), 312-319.

Song, Young In (1986). Battered Korean women in urban America: The relationship of cultural conflict to wife abuse. *Dissertation Abstracts International,* Nov., v47 (5-A), 1,883.

Sue, Stanley and Nolan, Zane (1987). The role of culture and cultural techniques in psychotherapy: A critique and reformulation. *American Psychologist,* v2 (1), 37-45.

Tatum, Beverly Daniel (1992). Talking about race, learning about racism: The application of racial identity development theory in the classroom. *Harvard Educational Review,* v62 (1), 1-24.

Torres, Sara (1991). A comparison of wife abuse between two cultures: Perceptions, attitudes, nature, and extent. Special Issue: Psychiatric nursing for the 1990s: New concepts, new therapies. *Issues in Mental Health Nursing,* Jan.-Mar., v12 (1), 113-131.

Uzzell, Odell and Peebles-Wilkins, Wilma (1989). Black spouse abuse: A focus on relational factors and intervention strategies. *Western Journal of Black Studies,* Spring, v13 (1), 10-16.

CHAPTER TEN

A Stalking Prevention Program

The author, in conjunction with Dr. Lenore Walker of Walker and Associates in Denver, Colorado, has developed a stalking prevention program for men who have been ordered by the court to stay away from their partners and placed on an electronic monitoring system to ensure compliance. (See Walker and Sonkin, 1994.) The primary goal of this program is to help men learn to control impulses toward stalking behaviors and thereby comply with court orders to stay away from the partner. This program is short-term in duration (no more than twelve weeks) because the men who are referred for this type of counseling are often waiting to go to trial on criminal charges. The stalking prevention program provides methods for addressing the unique needs of this particular population of male batterers, while also preparing these individuals for longer-term treatment and education programs, such as Learning to Live without Violence, should they be ordered into such treatment by the courts.

Along with Learning to Live without Violence, cognitive therapy provides the primary methodology that is used in the stalking prevention program. Both approaches are designed to be problem-focused and short-term in nature, and have been shown to be very effective with individuals who are experiencing mood disorders. Many batterers demonstrate extreme dependence and need of their partner, and have a history of overstepping interpersonal boundaries. These dependency needs are highlighted when the men are separated from their partners. As a result the men may express extreme depression and anxiety. In order to avoid overwhelming feelings of anxiety, dependency, loss, and rejection, men will often act out their need to feel in control by stalking and harassing their partner.

The stalking prevention program differs from other batterer treatment program models in being specifically designed to identify and break the dysfunctional thought processes that contribute to over-dependency and intrusive behavior patterns. It serves as an initial step to preventing stalking as well as stopping the other forms of physical, sexual, and psychological violence. Elements of the program are specified further on in this chapter.

STALKING DEFINED

As mentioned earlier, *stalking* includes any attempt on the perpetrator's behalf to follow, watch, harass, terrorize, or otherwise contact his partner against her desires. These contacts include in-person, telephone or mail contact, or communications through other persons. Stalking also includes any specific threats to kill or otherwise harm her, as well as veiled threats to kill or harm. Stalking may also include mailing cards or other cryptic messages, breaking windows or vandalizing her property including the car, taking away her mail, leaving things, such as flowers, on her doorstep or at work, watching her from afar, hang-ups on the telephone, or any other kinds of harassing behaviors.

In California, a recent law was passed broadening the definition of stalking, which allowed police greater discretion in making arrests of stalkers. This new law defines stalking as willful, malicious, and repeated following or harassing of another person, and making a credible threat with the intent to place that person in reasonable fear for his or her safety, or the safety of his or her immediate family. According to California law, *harassing* means a knowing and willful course of conduct directed at the specific person which seriously alarms, annoys, torments, or terrorizes the person and which serves no legitimate purpose. *Credible threat,* according to this new law, means a verbal or written threat, or a threat implied by a pattern of conduct made with the intent and the apparent ability to carry out the threat, so as to cause the person who is the target of the threat to reasonably fear for his or her safety or the safety of his or her family. *Course of conduct* is defined in the new law as meaning a pattern of conduct composed of a series of acts over a period of time, however short, evidencing a continuity of purpose.

COGNITIVE INTERVENTION STRATEGIES

As described earlier, studies have suggested that many male batterers may be suffering from a disorder of attachment that contributes to high levels of dysphoric mood states, such as anxiety or depression. When his partner leaves or wants a separation, the men find this situation very threatening. Getting her to return is one way of managing extreme emotional dysphoria and is an attempt to soothe himself. Another typical method that a batterer uses during a separation process is to try to reduce anxiety, depression, anger, etc., by persuading his partner to reconsider the separation. Communication may take place by talking to her over the telephone or in person, writing her, or getting in touch through friends or family members, regardless of the restraining order's terms. During this time men are particularly vulnerable to stalking their partner.

Cognitive therapy has been found to be very effective in the treatment of mood disorders. Cognitive interventions proposed in the stalking prevention program are specifically directed towards dysfunctional thinking processes that serve to escalate anxiety, anger, and the need to reattach to the partner as a means to quell emotional dysphoria. The interventions are geared toward teaching men how to soothe their own feelings resulting from the loss or separation rather than looking to external factors (their partner) to achieve this goal. These interventions may also be directed to the batterer's focus on eating, sleeping, working, and other daily routines that can help him better cope with the emotional ups and downs of the separation process. In addition to the cognitive interventions, the man may be introduced to many of the educational concepts and behavioral techniques that are included in many batterer treatment programs.

"CAN THIS RELATIONSHIP BE SAVED?"

During the initial stages of intervention, it is critical for the batterer not to feel stripped of all hope that his relationship and family will ever be put back together, even though a realistic appraisal of the situation is important, too. For example, saying to the batterer, "You have absolutely lost your family," before he has developed mechanisms to deal with this loss (no matter how true it might appear to the counselor from contact with the victim), can predictably escalate his dysfunctional thought processes and subsequent destructive behavior. Instead, it is more beneficial for the counselor to acknowledge the client's goal to get back with his family as legitimate, while defining his current methods for accomplishing this goal as likely to only increase the possibility of escalating the problem. Further, it is pointed out that to follow, harass, watch, stalk, coerce, intimidate, threaten, or manipulate her into returning undermines the ultimate goal of saving the relationship. The man needs to know that he probably will get an opportunity to talk to his wife to plead his case, but he must first get his life under control so that she may actually want to talk to him and seriously consider what he has to say without being coerced or intimidated. Of course, the counselor should not guarantee any particular outcome with regard to his relationship, even if the batterer does everything exactly as he is taught. Similarly, the victim must not be encouraged to provide the rewards for the batterer's changed behavior. Instead, the counselor must help the batterer to want to change because appropriate and responsible behavior will provide the best chance to obtain his short-term and long-term goals.

THE SPECIFIC INTERVENTIONS

Defining stalking. An important step in helping men learn to control impulses to stalk is their learning the definition of stalking, the reasons why men stalk, and how to identify dysfunctional thought patterns that contribute to impulses to stalk and abuse their partner.

Current adaptive coping skills. Before you present the cognitive theory, it is helpful to explore cognitive and behavioral techniques the man may already employ to control his anxiety and depression resulting from the separation. This exercise will also get men to begin to make the connection between thoughts and feelings, and understand how they interact to influence behavior. The counselor wants to build upon the client's current adaptive coping mechanisms.

Cognitive therapy theory. Thoughts and feelings reflect our core selves and are expressed via our behaviors — how we interact with the world. The premise of cognitive theory — although recognizing the synergistic relationship between behavior, cognitions, and affect — states that the best method to intervene in changing psychological problems is through altering the cognitions rather than focusing on the emotions (Beck, 1976). Many cognitive therapists also incorporate behavioral interventions in order to bring about a change in behaviors (Persons, 1989). The main focus of cognitive interventions is changing dysfunctional thought processes that ultimately contribute to anxiety, depression and other emotional and behavioral problems (Beck, Emery, and Greenberg, 1985; Beck, Rush, Shaw, and Emery, 1979).

There are three common types of dysfunctional thought patterns that contribute to a batterer's feeling emotionally overwhelmed by the separation:

1. Thoughts that reflect negative beliefs about self or others

2. Maladaptive thoughts that ultimately serve to escalate or exacerbate dysphoric mood states

3. Irrational thought patterns that do not reflect reality and also serve to escalate or exacerbate dysphoric mood states

These three types of thought patterns are not mutually exclusive — there is some overlap. However, they are presented individually to begin to help clients learn to identify the various ways in which they escalate their feelings during the separation period and in so doing make themselves vulnerable to stalking.

Thoughts that reflect negative beliefs about self or others. These thoughts relate to global core beliefs about oneself or others. From an attachment point of view, these thoughts represent a person's perception of himself — that is, his personal sense of worthiness (e.g., "Am I lovable?"). These thoughts also represent one's perception or schema of others — that is, the other's trustworthiness or reliability (e.g., "Will I be rejected?) (Bowlby, 1977). Male batterers typically view themselves as either unworthy of love, untrusting that others won't reject them, or both. The following are examples of this type of dysfunctional thought pattern that male batterers often experience during a separation:

- "I will not survive without her."

- "She will never trust me again."

- "I am worthless for abusing her."

- "She is going to abandon me."

- "If I tell her how I feel, she will use it against me."

These and similar thoughts speak to the core of our expectations of the batterer and his partner. These statements are likely to become self-fulfilled prophesies, in that if he believes that he cannot trust others he will find reasons for distrust. Likewise, if he believes that he is worthless, he will find evidence for lack of worth. Although these thought patterns do reflect an inner reality, they rarely reflect the outer reality.

Maladaptive thoughts that ultimately serve to escalate or exacerbate dysphoric mood states. These types of thought patterns, unlike the previous category, may on the surface appear rational, logical, and realistic, but upon closer examination are negative in that they only serve to escalate dysphoric mood states. In their extreme form, they can be obsessive and externalizing thought patterns that are very difficult to stop.

The following are examples of these types of thought patterns:

- "This is all her fault."

- "If she didn't leave, we could work things out together."

- "Her counselor is the one who got her to leave me."

- "If she hadn't called the police, we wouldn't be having these problems."

- "She'll never come back unless I do something."

- "I've got to get her back."

These and similar thoughts reinforce the batterer's belief that he is not responsible for his problems — that rather his partner and others are responsible for what is now happening to him. They also keep his focus on getting her to return rather than addressing his own problems which caused the separation in the first place. Breaking the pattern of externalizing responsibility is not only necessary to prevent stalking behaviors, but also to stop all forms of violence.

Irrational thought patterns that do not reflect reality. These thoughts reflect an unrealistic appraisal of oneself or others. This is frequently a result of the man letting his feelings define his reality. The most common forms of this type of pattern are paranoid thinking, all-or-nothing thinking, catastrophizing, and thoughts of revenge.

The following are examples of these types of thought patterns:

- "She has probably been planning to leave me for another man for years."

- "If she doesn't return now, she will never return."

- "She is getting everyone to be against me; the whole world will soon know my problems."

- "I have to teach her a lesson, otherwise she will never believe me that I love her."

Each of these statements represents the core fear that many batterers experience — abandonment. The person who thinks these thoughts is no doubt going to experience increased depression or anxiety which ultimately may result in strong desires to make contact, force a premature reconciliation, or cause physical harm. These thoughts may be particularly dangerous when they focus on sexual infidelity. The identification of these types of thoughts may lead the counselor to evaluate the potential lethality of a particular client as discussed in Chapter Seven.

In summary, all forms of dysfunctional thought patterns only serve to escalate negative affect. Therefore, when stalkers seek to control their partner it is usually in an effort to gain control over these overwhelming emotions. It is their hope that by getting her to return, the feelings will subside. The connection between the negative thoughts and the strong feelings is rarely within the man's awareness. For most men the motivation is to just get her back. Identifying the dysfunctional thought patterns is a first important step to preventing the stalking behaviors. By breaking the dysfunctional thought patterns, in conjunction with other psychoeducational techniques, batterers can feel less overwhelmed by the realities of the separation and therefore better control their impulses and their immediate need for reconciliation. In this way the batterer can focus on solving his violence problem and be in a better position to earn her trust should she decide to give the relationship another chance.

Identifying dysfunctional thoughts. Before breaking dysfunctional thought patterns that contribute to stalking behaviors, the counselor must be willing to point out the dysfunctional thoughts and assist the client in understanding how those thoughts escalate negative affect. In addition, the counselor must be specific rather than discuss the problem generally or in theory. It is suggested that counselors ask questions in order to understand the client's dysfunctional thought process and, in doing so, highlight the dysfunctional thought patterns. For example:

Client: I have to get in touch with her.

Therapist: What will happen if you don't get in touch with her?

Client: She will find another man.

Therapist: What makes you think she will find another man?

Client: She'll want to be with someone.

Therapist: What will happen to you if she does get together with another man?

Client: I'll go nuts.

Therapist: What will happen then?

Client: I'll never get over it.

Therapist: And so if she left you for another man, you would *never* get over it. Is that really true about yourself? What makes you think you would never get over it?

Client: It would hurt so much.

Therapist: This is true, it will hurt, but aren't you playing out the future a bit too much right now? More importantly, I wonder what effect your thinking that you will never get over it has on your feelings today?

Thought journal. There are a number of techniques for identifying dysfunctional thought patterns. The primary technique is the thought journal, a daily record of the client's thoughts, feelings, and behaviors and the positive coping mechanisms for counteracting the negative effects of the dysfunctional thought patterns. Completing the thought journal helps the client develop a greater awareness of, and ultimately change, his dysfunctional thought patterns. First, by naming the type of dysfunctional thought pattern, the client begins to differentiate when he is experiencing negative global thoughts, maladaptive thoughts, or irrational thoughts. The second rationale for the thought journal is that the client can learn to recognize how his dysfunctional thoughts ultimately affect his feelings and behaviors. Lastly, the client, by working in the journal, gets practice at challenging his thoughts so as to soothe his anxiety or depression. The client is encouraged to complete at least one entry per day during the entire intervention program. Although this may seem like a lot of work, for most clients, one entry per day is only the tip of the iceberg when it comes to dysfunctional thinking.

Challenging dysfunctional thoughts. The process of challenging thoughts involves questioning the validity of the thoughts, looking for alternative explanations, and encouraging thoughts that calm, soothe, and reassure. Other methods of challenging these thoughts include applying humor and learning about the origin of the thought patterns. Most importantly, the counselor must help the client be as specific as possible about what he thinks so as to reveal the dysfunctional thought patterns. The client ultimately needs to see how certain thought patterns reflect and reinforce negative attitudes about self and/or others, do not reflect reality, or are simply maladaptive in that they subsequently exacerbate negative affect and put him at risk for acting out. Awareness of these patterns is a first and important step in this process. Challenging these thought patterns can redirect a client's focus from struggling with impulses to changing beliefs that contribute to those tendencies.

Talking it out. For some men, having a safe place to identify and talk about their feelings about the separation may provide the necessary structure and release of pressure to prevent acting out in the form of stalking or other harassing behavior. However, for other men, talking in counseling may provide only short-term relief from the anxiety, and afterwards the emotional dysphoria may return making him vulnerable to feeling overwhelmed and subsequently acting out. At this time, we have no way of differentiating who is and who is not at risk for stalking. Therefore, it is critical that all men are given specific directives as to how to control dysphoric mood states between sessions.

A WORD OF CAUTION

Although mental health professionals are not able to predict violent behavior with any degree of accuracy with the patient population in general, domestic violence clients are one exception to this rule. This is because the best predictor of future behavior is past behavior. The vast majority of domestic violence defendants who enter into the criminal justice system already have a history of violent behavior directed towards their current partner or previous partners. Therefore, we can say with a certain amount of certainty that, short of any interventions, the client will continue to batter his partner. Similarly, research has indicated that violence will not only reoccur in the future, but it is likely to occur with greater frequency and severity. As a rule, a safe approach to assessing a client for participation in any domestic violence prevention program is that the greater the current potential lethality, the greater the need for limits and restraints. Therefore, it is recommended that intervention programs are for individuals who *do not* pose an immediate lethal threat to their partner.

Fifteen years ago, the San Francisco Family Violence Project (now called the Family Violence Prevention Fund) conducted a study of approximately three hundred police incident reports to scan narratives for reasons for the argument that eventually led to the domestic violence incident. The most frequently stated reason for the argument and the subsequent violence was the discussion of separation and divorce. This study supported the many anecdotal reports received since that time that, during periods of separation and when the woman files for divorce (or just the discussion of either), the woman is at greater risk for violence. The newspapers are full of stories of domestic homicides that occur under these circumstances. Therefore, counselors should be acutely aware of the extremely high danger inherent in men during this difficult period. Unfortunately there is no research on this particular population of male batterers; therefore, we have no idea as to how long it may take to stabilize a man who is at risk for stalking. Counselors will need to assess on a case-by-case basis as to when a man is ready to progress to another stage in the process of treatment.

REFERENCES

Beck, Aaron T. (1976). *Cognitive therapy and the emotional disorders.* New York: International Universities Press.

Beck, Aaron T.; Rush, A.J.; Shaw, B.F.; and Emery, G. (1979). *Cognitive therapy of depression.* New York: Guilford Publications.

Beck, Aaron T.; Emery, Gary; and Greenberg, Ruth L. (1985). *Anxiety disorders and phobias: A cognitive perspective.* New York: Basic Books.

Bowlby, J. (1977). The making and breaking of affectional bonds. *British Journal of Psychiatry,* 92, 196-209.

Persons, Jacqueline (1989). *Cognitive therapy in practice: A case formulation approach.* New York: W.W. Norton & Co., Inc.

Walker, L.E.A. and Sonkin, D.J. (1994). *JurisMonitor stabilization and empowerment programs.* Denver, CO: Endolar Publications.

EPILOGUE

A Final Word to the Reader

This book has described the orientation I have used and have found to be successful with many male batterers, which was outlined in my first book, *Learning to Live without Violence: A Handbook for Men* (1989 rev.), while at the same time presenting an unbiased examination of other approaches to counseling this population. It has only been twenty years since, as a society, we began to recognize the seriousness and prevalence of the problem of domestic violence. The psychology profession has lagged behind in this awareness some five or ten years; therefore, mental health professionals are only just beginning to understand the male batterer and how to treat him.

It appears that criminal justice sanctions, although critically important, are not enough to bring about changes in men's violent behaviors. Some form of treatment is necessary for most male batterers to break the cycle of violence in their lives. How this treatment takes form may not be as important as men receiving new skills and education — and the hope that it is possible to live a life without violence. Although there are many different approaches (as well as variations within each approach) to treatment (cognitive-behavioral, feminist, and family systems, to name a few), various modalities (individual, group, couple/family), and differing lengths of treatment (short-, medium- and long-term), the consistent thread that runs through them all is the counselor's genuine desire to break the cycle of domestic violence. No matter what approach one may examine, the counselor's stance is against violence. Even though some of the counseling approaches are driven by radically different philosophies, counselors are struggling to develop treatment interventions that are effective for the population with whom they are working. Because the problem of domestic violence is so pervasive, common sense would dictate that a variety of approaches may ultimately be needed to address the diverse needs of a large segment of society.

Because of the ever-present potential for danger toward others, counselors are likely to encounter situations in their treatment of male batterers where they may be required to act in order to protect others. Therefore, it is critical that persons working with this population, whether professionally trained or not, receive education that will help him or her make better, more informed, clinical decisions. I recommend the following actions be taken by any person working with this population.

1. Clinical consultation on a regular basis to discuss assessment and intervention strategies.

2. Clinical education by attending conferences and workshops that will help counselors update their knowledge and skills. Similarly, it is also important to peruse research journals devoted to the study of interpersonal violence such as *Violence and Victims* or the *Journal of Interpersonal Violence*.

3. Continuing education on legal and ethical issues relating to the mental health profession. Because of the high risk inherent in working with domestic violence perpetrators, it would be equally important for clinicians to attend workshops or conferences, or read books or journal articles on the assessment of dangerousness, mandatory reporting laws, and other legal and ethical responsibilities.

In addition to continuing education, I strongly urge persons working on this issue to network on a regular basis with other service providers, researchers, and advocates in your community in order to decrease isolation and burnout — and most importantly to facilitate a dialogue between persons with a similar goal in mind: to end family violence. I encourage persons working with this population to not get too narrowly focused on your own ideas or get caught up in the dogma of what is politically correct with regard to treatment. Instead, in reading the literature you will find that highly skilled and committed individuals are making valuable contributions to our knowledge of domestic violence. Their ideas and suggestions may help give your approach greater depth and the ability to respond to the needs of a wider range of perpetrators. Similarly, there is much to learn from other disciplines, such as developmental psychology and those dealing with child abuse, trauma and chemical dependency, to name a few. Cross-fertilization of disciplines can not only broaden our understanding of the most effective treatment interventions, but also elucidate the causes of violence and how we may work to prevent the next generation from repeating the mistakes of this and prior ones.

In addition to evaluating the most effective philosophy of treatment intervention, there will need to be greater exploration as to the length of treatment exposure necessary to bring about an end of violent behaviors. The vast majority of programs have been developed as short-term interventions (six months or less). Although some men will greatly benefit from such programs, the offender who has a long-term pattern of violence and poor social problem-solving skills may need to keep in contact with a program for many years. We have yet to develop extensive and easily accessible long-term assistance programs for men in need of continued support.

Another important issue, yet to be fully elucidated, is for clinicians to better understand the transmission of violent behaviors from a physiological, developmental, and social perspective. The relationship between witnessing family violence and later perpetration of violence is now being clearly documented; however, the exact mode of transmission (physiological, psychological, and social) is yet to be understood. Such data will not only be useful in treating adult and adolescent offenders, but also in treating child victims/witnesses of violence and in developing social policy regarding the intervention and prevention of child abuse and neglect as well.

Most importantly, I urge service providers to not become too entrenched in your own perspective because, ultimately, a client will come along who does not fit into your mold. Just as not all persons will favorably respond to one antidepressant medication, not all batterers will favorably respond to one type of intervention. The following is a case in point.

I was referred a twenty-one-year-old man who had participated in a batterers program in a neighboring county, but for some reason had continued to batter his wife, who was also twenty-one years old. I worked with him individually, primarily using the program outlined in *Learning to Live without Violence*, on the condition that he continue to participate in the batterers program. Each week he would describe continued acts of violence at the beginning of the session. He would describe these acts as if someone else was perpetrating them. He expressed concern but not any great worry about his continued violence. His wife refused to attend a local battered women's support group, but I was able to meet with her on a number of occasions during my assessment process. I referred her to individual counseling but she refused to go. Like him, she also expressed concern but not any overt worry about the chronic violence. Both had family in the area that were aware of the problems between them; however, neither family was directly involved with their situation.

After about six sessions — reporting continued violence each week — I became increasingly concerned about either the man or woman being seriously injured. I spoke with his counselor at the local batterers program, who was also feeling at wit's end as to what to do at this point. In speaking with my peer consultation group, I described this man and woman as acting like young children unable to get along with each other, the only difference being that one of these "children" was likely to kill the other. I began to find myself daily worrying about when I was going to read in the newspaper about one of them killing the other. Then I asked myself, "Why am I the one doing all the worrying? In fact, their families should also be worrying." At that moment, I had an idea — what about family therapy? I decided to bring in both families and conduct sessions with all family members on both sides.

The response was immediate. The period between the session when I met with both the man and woman to tell them of the new treatment plan, and the session with all available family members, was the first week in seven weeks when the man didn't report any physical, sexual, or psychological violence. By reframing this situation into a family therapy case, I was able to shift the worry from me to the man, his wife, and their respective families. Ten years ago, when I was espousing the evils of couples and family therapy with domestic violence, I never would have allowed myself to find an alternative approach to my typical treatment interventions with male batterers. I probably would have written this off to the client's lack of motivation to change rather than lack of creativity on my behalf.

We are still in the infant stages of the field of domestic violence. This is especially true with regard to our understanding the psychology of the offender. However, there is much to borrow from other clinical and research disciplines. What is most needed is greater cooperation between the sociopolitical, service delivery, and research communities. Much is known about human behavior, and although domestic violence activists may believe this is a unique issue, we share much in common with others working in other areas of psychology and social issues. It is not necessary to reinvent the wheel, but only to tailor it to fit our particular vehicle.

Suggested Reading

This is not an exhaustive review of the literature on treatment of male batterers, but rather a list of books and journal articles that I have personally reviewed and found helpful in addressing the various issues in this book. I may have inadvertently left out additional excellent materials on this topic. My apology to other authors.

DOMESTIC VIOLENCE AND TREATMENT OF MALE BATTERERS

American Psychiatric Association (1994). *Diagnostic and statistical manual of mental disorders: Fourth edition (DSM-IV).* Washington, DC: American Psychiatric Association.

Adams, D.C. (1986). *Counseling men who batter: A profeminist analysis of clinical models.* Paper presented at the Annual Meeting of the American Psychiatric Association, May 14, 1986.

Ammerman, Robert T. and Hersen, Michel (eds.) (1990). *Treatment of family violence: A sourcebook.* New York: John Wiley and Sons.

Ammerman, Robert T. and Hersen, Michel (eds.) (1991). *Case studies in family violence.* New York: Plenum Publishing.

Beavers, W. Robert and Hampton, Robert B. (1993). Measuring family competence: The Beavers Systems Model. In: Froma Walsh (ed.), *Normal family processes* (2nd ed.). Guilford family therapy series. New York: Guilford Publications, pp. 73-103.

Beck, Aaron T. (1976). *Cognitive therapy and the emotional disorders.* New York: International Universities Press.

Beck, Aaron T.; Rush, A.J.; Shaw, B.F.; and Emery, G. (1979). *Cognitive therapy of depression.* New York: Guilford Publications.

Beck, Aaron T.; Emery, Gary; and Greenberg, Ruth L. (1985). *Anxiety disorders and phobias: A cognitive perspective.* New York: Basic Books.

Bograd, M. (1984). Family systems approaches to wife battering: A feminist critique. *American Journal of Orthopsychiatry*, 54 (4), 558-568.

Bowlby, J. (1977). The making and breaking of affectional bonds. *British Journal of Psychiatry*, 92, 196-209.

Browne, A. (1987). *When battered women kill.* New York: Free Press.

Burman, Bonnie; John, Richard S.; and Margolin, Gayla (1992). Observed patterns of conflict in violent, nonviolent, and nondistressed couples. *Behavioral Assessment*, Spring, v14 (n1), 15-37.

Burman, Bonnie; Margolin, Gayla; and John, Richard S. (1993). America's angriest home videos: Behavioral contingencies observed in home reenactments of marital conflict. Special Section: Couples and couple therapy. *Journal of Consulting & Clinical Psychology*, Feb., v61 (n1), 28-39.

Caesar, P.L. (1985). *The male batterer: Personality and psychosocial characteristics.* Unpublished doctoral dissertation, California School of Professional Psychology, Berkeley, CA.

Caesar, P. Lynn and Hamberger, L. Kevin (eds.) (1989). *Treating men who batter: Theory, practice and programs.* New York: Springer Publications.

Dutton, D. (1986). The outcome of court-mandated treatment for wife assault: A quasi-experimental evaluation. *Violence and Victims*, 1 (3), 163-176.

Dutton, D.G. (1988, rev. 1995). *The domestic assault of women: Psychological and criminal justice perspectives.* Boston: Allyn & Bacon, Inc.

Dutton, D.G.; Bodnarchuk, M.; Kropp, R.; Hart, S.; and Ogloff, J. (1994). *A ten-year follow-up of court-mandated wife assault treatment.* Vancouver, BC: British Columbia Institute of Family Violence.

Dutton, D.G.; Saunders, K.; Starzomski, A.; and Batholomew, K. (1994). Intimacy-anger and insecure attachment as precursors of abuse in intimate relationships. *Journal of Applied Social Psychology*, 24 (15), 1367-1386.

Edleson, Jeffrey L. and Tolman, Richard M. (1992). *Intervention for men who batter: An ecological approach.* Newbury Park, CA: Sage Publications, Inc.

Elbow, M. (1977). Theoretical considerations of violent marriages. *Social Casework*, Oct., v63 (8), 465-471.

Everstine, D.S. and Everstine, L. (1993). *The trauma response: Treatment for emotional injury.* New York: W.W. Norton & Co., Inc.

Farley, Dennis and Magill, Judith (1988). An evaluation of a group program for men who batter. Special Issue: Violence: Prevention and treatment in groups. *Social Work with Groups*, 11 (3), 53-65.

Ganley, A. (1981). *Court-mandated counseling for men who batter* (participants and trainers manuals). Washington, DC: The Center for Women's Policy Studies.

Ganley, A. (1987). Perpetrators of domestic violence: An overview of counseling the court-mandated client. In: D.J. Sonkin (ed.), *Domestic violence on trial: Psychological and legal dimensions of family violence.* New York: Springer Publications.

Ganley, A. and Harris, L. (1978). *Domestic violence: Issues in designing and implementing programs for male batterers.* Paper presented at the 86th Annual Convention of the American Psychological Association, Toronto, Canada.

Geffner, R. and Mantooth, C. (1989). A psychoeducational conjoint therapy approach to reducing family violence. In: P.L. Caesar and L.K. Hamberger (eds.), *Treating men who batter: Theory, practice and programs.* New York: Springer Publications.

Gelles, Richard and Straus, Murray (1988). *Intimate violence: The definitive study of the causes and consequences of abuse in the American family.* New York: Simon and Schuster.

Gondolf, Edward W. (1988). How some men stop their abuse: An exploratory program evaluation. In: Gerald T. Hotaling, David Finkelhor, John T. Kirkpatrick, and Murray A. Straus (eds.), *Coping with family violence: Research and policy perspectives.* Newbury Park, CA: Sage Publications, Inc., pp. 129-144.

Gondolf, Edward (1988). *Research on men who batter: An overview, bibliography and resource guide.* Bradenton, FL: Human Services Institute, Inc.

Gondolf, Edward and Russell, David (1987). *Man to man: A guide for men in abusive relationships.* Brandenton, FL: Human Services Institute, Inc.

Hastings, J. and Hamberger, L.K. (1988). Personality characteristics of spouse abusers: A controlled comparison. *Violence and Victims,* Spring, v3 (1), 31-48.

Hotaling, G.T. and Sugerman, D.B. (1986). An analysis of risk markers in husband to wife violence: The current state of knowledge. *Violence and Victims,* 1 (2), 101-124.

Jenkins, Alan (1990). *Invitations to responsibility: The therapeutic engagement of men who are violent and abusive.* Adelaide, South Australia: Dulwich Centre Publications.

Koss, M.; Goodman, L.; Fitzgerald, L.; Russo, N.F.; Keita, G.P.; and Browne, A. (1994). *No safe haven: Male violence against women at home, at work and in the community.* Washington, DC: American Psychological Association.

Lane, G. and Russell, T. (1989). Second-order systemic work with violent couples. In: P.L. Caesar and L.K. Hamberger (eds.), *Treating men who batter: Theory, practice and programs.* New York: Springer Publications.

Madanes, Cloe (1990). *Sex, love and violence: Strategies for transformation.* New York: W.W. Norton & Co., Inc.

Mantooth, C.M.; Geffner, R.; Franks, D.; and Patrick, J. (1987). *Family violence: A treatment manual for reducing couple violence.* Tyler, TX: University of Texas at Tyler Press.

Margolin, Gayla and Burman, Bonnie (1993). Wife abuse versus marital violence: Different terminologies, explanations, and solutions. Special Issue: Marital conflict. *Clinical Psychology Review,* v13 (n1), 59-73.

Martin, Del (1976, rev. 1981). *Battered wives.* Volcano, CA: Volcano Press.

McKay, Matthew; Rogers, Peter; and McKay, Judith (1989). *When anger hurts: Quieting the storm within.* Oakland, CA: New Harbinger Publications.

Neidig, P. and Freidman, D. (1986). *Domestic violence containment: A spouse abuse treatment program.* Urbana, IL: Research Press.

Paymar, Michael (1993). *Violent no more: Helping men end domestic abuse.* Alameda, CA: Hunter House.

Pense, Ellen and Paymar, Michael (1993). *Education groups for men who batter: The Duluth Model.* New York: Springer Publications.

Persons, Jacqueline (1989). *Cognitive therapy in practice: A case formulation approach.* New York: W.W. Norton & Co., Inc.

Poynter, Tracey L. (1989). An evaluation of a group programme for male perpetrators of domestic violence. *Australian Journal of Sex, Marriage & Family,* 10 (3), 133-142.

Saunders, D. (1987). *Are there three different types of men who batter? An empirical study with possible implications for treatment.* Paper presented at the Third National Family Violence Research Conference. July 6-9, Durham, New Hampshire.

Saunders, D.G. (1989). Cognitive and behavioral interventions with men who batter: Applications and outcomes. In: P.L. Caesar and L.K. Hamberger (eds.), *Treating men who batter: Theory, practice and programs.* New York: Springer Publications.

Scharff, David E. and Scharff, Jill Savege (1991). Object relations couple therapy. Northvale, NJ: Jason Aronson, Inc.

Sherman, L.W. and Berk, R.A. (1984). The specific deterrent effects of arrest for domestic violence. *American Sociological Review,* 49, 261-272.

Shields, N.M.; McCall, G.J.; and Hanneke, C.R. (1988). Patterns of family and nonfamily violence: Violent husbands and violent men. *Violence and Victims,* Summer, v3 (2), 83-98.

Sonkin, D.J. (ed.) (1987). *Domestic violence on trial: Psychological and legal dimensions of family violence.* New York: Springer Publications.

Sonkin, D.J. (1987). The assessment of court-mandated male batterers. In: D.J. Sonkin (ed.), *Domestic violence on trial: Psychological and legal dimensions of family violence.* New York: Springer Publications.

Sonkin, D.J. (1992). *Wounded men: A man's guide to recovering from child abuse.* Stamford, CT: Long Meadow Press.

Sonkin, D.J. and Durphy, M. (1982, rev. 1989). *Learning to live without violence: A handbook for men.* Volcano, CA: Volcano Press.

Sonkin, D.J.; Martin, D.; and Walker, L.E.A. (1985). *The male batterer: A treatment approach.* New York: Springer Publications.

Steinmetz, S.K. and Straus, M. (1974). *Violence in the family.* New York: Harper and Row.

Straus, M.A.; Gelles, R.J.; and Steinmetz, S.K. (1980). *Behind closed doors: Violence in the American family.* New York: Anchor-Doubleday.

Stordeur, R.A. and Stille, R. (1989). *Ending men's violence against their partners: One road to peace.* Newbury Park, CA: Sage Publications, Inc.

Tolman, R.M. (1989). The development of a measure of psychological maltreatment of women by their male partners. *Violence and Victims,* Fall, v4 (3), 159-178.

Walker, L.E.A. (1979). *The battered woman.* New York: Harper and Row.

Walker, L.E. (1985). *The battered woman syndrome.* New York: Springer Publications.

Walker, L.E. (1989). *Terrifying love: Why battered women kill and how society responds.* New York: Harper and Row.

Walker, L.E.A. (1994). *Abused women and survivor therapy: A practical guide for the psychotherapist.* Washington, DC: APA Press.

Walker, L.E.A. and Sonkin, D.J. (1994). *JurisMonitor stabilization and empowerment programs.* Denver, CO: Endolar Publications.

CHILD WITNESSES TO SPOUSAL VIOLENCE

Brassard, M.R.; Germain, R.; and Hart, S.N. (1987). *Psychological maltreatment of children and youth.* New York: Pergamon Press.

Brassard, M.R.; Hart, S.N.; and Hardy, D.B. (1993). The psychological maltreatment rating scales. *Child Abuse and Neglect,* v17 (6), 715-730.

Doumas, Diana; Margolin, Gayla; and John, Richard S. (1994). The intergenerational transmission of aggression across three generations. *Journal of Family Violence,* Jun., v9 (n2), 157-175.

Eth, Spencer and Pynoos, Robert (1985). *Post-traumatic stress disorder in children*. Washington, DC: American Psychiatric Press.

Goodman, G.S. and Rosenberg, M.S. (1987). *The child witness to family violence: Clinical and legal considerations*. In: D.J. Sonkin (ed.), *Domestic violence on trial: Psychological and legal dimensions of family violence*. New York: Springer Publications.

Jaffe, Peter G.; Wolfe, David A.; and Wilson, Susan K. (1990). *Children of battered women*. Newbury Park, CA: Sage Publications, Inc.

Johnson, Kendall (1989). *Trauma in the lives of children: Crisis and stress management techniques for counselors and other professionals*. Alameda, CA: Hunter House.

McCann, Lisa and Pearlman, Laurie (1990). *Psychological trauma and the adult survivor: Theory, therapy and transformation*. New York: Brunner/Mazel Publishers.

Rosenberg, M.S. (1987). Children of battered women: The effects of witnessing violence on their social problem-solving abilities. *Behavior Therapist*, v10 (4), 85-89.

Van der Kolk, B. (1987). *Psychological trauma*. Washington, DC: American Psychiatric Press.

Wohl, Agnes and Kaufman, Bobbie (1985). *Silent screams and hidden cries: An interpretation of artwork by children from violent families*. New York: Brunner/Mazel Publishers.

ETHNICITY AND DOMESTIC VIOLENCE

Anderson, Louis P. (1991). Acculturative stress: A theory of relevance to Black Americans. *Clinical Psychology Review*, v11 (n6), 685-702.

Bell, Carl C. and Chance-Hill, Gerri (1991). Treatment of violent families. Annual Meeting of the American Family Therapy Association (1988, Montreal, Canada). *Journal of the National Medical Association*, Mar., v83 (3), 203-208.

Black Bear, Tillie (1988). Native American clients. In: Anne L. Horton and Judith A. Williamson (eds.), *Abuse and religion: When praying isn't enough*. Lexington, MA: Lexington Books/D.C. Heath and Company, pp. 135-136.

Boone, Sherle L. (1991). Aggression in African-American boys: A discriminant analysis. *Genetic, Social, & General Psychology Monographs*, May, v117 (2), 203-228.

Brice-Baker, Janet R. (1994). Domestic violence in African-American and African-Caribbean families. Special Issue: Multicultural views on domestic violence. *Journal of Social Distress & the Homeless*, Jan., v3 (1), 23-38.

Burns, M.C. (ed.) (1986). *The speaking profits us: Violence in the lives of women of color.* Seattle, WA: Center for the Prevention of Sexual and Domestic Violence.

Campbell, Doris Williams; Campbell, Jacquelyn; King, Christine; Parker, Barbara; and Ryan, Josephine (1994). The reliability and factor structure of the index of spouse abuse with African-American women. *Violence and Victims,* v9 (3).

Canino, Ian A. and Spurlock, Jeanne (1994). *Culturally diverse children and adolescents: Assessment, diagnosis and treatment.* New York: Guilford Publications.

Comas-Diaz, Lillian and Greene, Beverly (1994). *Women of color: Integrating ethnic and gender identities in psychotherapy.* New York: Guilford Publications.

Daniel, Jessica H.; Hampton, Robert L.; and Newberger, Eli H. (1983). Child abuse and accidents in black families: A controlled comparative study. *American Journal of Orthopsychiatry,* Oct., v53 (4), 645-653.

DeBruyn, Lemyra M.; Hymbaugh, Karen; and Valdez, Norma (1988). Helping communities address suicide and violence: The Special Initiatives Team of the Indian Health Service. *American Indian & Alaska Native Mental Health Research,* Mar., v1 (3), 56-65.

Diaz, Daniel P. (1989). Hispanic and Anglo marital conflict resolution and marital violence. *Dissertation Abstracts International,* Jan., v49 (7-B), 2850.

Finn, Jerry (1986). The relationship between sex-role attitudes and attitudes supporting marital violence. *Sex Roles,* Mar., v14 (5-6), 235-244.

Frye, Barbara A. and D'Avanzo, Carolyn D. (1994). Cultural themes in family stress and violence among Cambodian refugee women in the inner city. *Advances in Nursing Science,* Mar., v16 (n3), 64-77.

Gaines, S.O. and Reed, E.S. (1995). Prejudice: From Allport to DuBois. *American Psychologist,* 50 (2), 96-103.

Gotowiec, Andrew and Beiser, Morton (1993-94). Aboriginal children's mental health: Unique challenges. *Canada's Mental Health,* Winter, v41 (4), 7-11.

Hampton, Robert L. (1977). Marital disruption among Blacks. *Dissertation Abstracts International,* Sep., v38 (3-A), 1685-1686.

Hampton, Robert L. (1987). *Violence in the Black family: Correlates and consequences.* Lexington, MA: Lexington Books/D.C. Heath and Company.

Hampton, Robert L. (1987). Race, class and child maltreatment. *Journal of Comparative Family Studies,* Spring, v18 (1), 113-126.

Hampton, Robert L. (1991). Child abuse in the African-American community. In: Joyce E. Everett, Sandra Stukes Chipungu, and Bogart R. Leashore (eds.), *Child welfare: An Africentric perspective.* New Brunswick, NJ: Rutgers University Press, pp. 220-246.

Ho, Christine K. (1990). An analysis of domestic violence in Asian-American communities: A multicultural approach to counseling. Special issue: Diversity and complexity in feminist therapy: I. *Women & Therapy,* v9 (n1-2), 129-150.

Kanuha, Valli (1994). Women of color in battering relationships. In: Lillian Comas-Dias and Beverly Greene (eds.), *Women of color: Integrating ethnic and gender identities in psychotherapy.* New York: Guilford Publications.

Larose, François (1989). L'environnement des réserves Indiennes est-il pathogene? Réflexions sur le suicide et l'identification des facteurs de risque en milieu Amerindien Québecois. (Is the environment of Indian reservations...) *Revue Québecoise de Psychologie,* v10 (1), 31-44.

Lockhart, Lettie L. (1985). Methodological issues in comparative racial analyses: The case of wife abuse. *Social Work Research & Abstracts,* Summer, v21 (2), 35-41.

Lockhart, Lettie L. (1987). A reexamination of the effects of race and social class on the incidence of marital violence: A search for reliable differences. *Journal of Marriage & the Family,* Aug., v49 (3), 603-610.

Lockhart, Lettie and White, Barbara W. (1989). Understanding marital violence in the black community. *Journal of Interpersonal Violence,* Dec., v4 (4), 421-436.

Marsh, Clifton E. (1993). Sexual assault and domestic violence in the African-American community. *Western Journal of Black Studies,* Fall, v17 (3), 149-155.

McGoldrick, Monica; Pearce, John K.; and Giordano, Joseph (eds.) (1982). *Ethnicity and family therapy.* New York: Guilford Publications.

Parilla, Julia L.; Bakeman, Roger; and Norris, Fran H. (1994). Culture and domestic violence: The ecology of abused Latinas. *Violence and Victims,* v9 (3).

Paulson, Morris J.; Coombs, Robert H.; and Landsverk, John (1990). Youth who physically assault their parents. *Journal of Family Violence,* Jun., v5 (2), 121-133.

Pedersen, Paul and Carey, John (1994). *Multicultural counseling in schools: A practical handbook.* New York: Allyn & Bacon, Inc.

Plass, Peggy S. (1993). African-American family homicide: Patterns in partner, parent, and child victimization, 1985-1987. *Journal of Black Studies,* Jun., v23 (4), 515-538.

Rodriguez, Vivianne (1986). Attitudes towards corporal punishment, social support system, and conflict resolution techniques related to family violence in Puerto Rican families living in the United States. *Dissertation Abstracts International,* Mar., v46 (9-A), 2635.

Roundtree, George A.; Parker, Archie D.; Edwards, Dan W.; and Teddlie, Charles B. (1982). A survey of the types of crimes committed by incarcerated females in two states who reported being battered. *Corrective & Social Psychiatry & Journal of Behavior Technology, Methods & Therapy,* v28 (1), 23-26.

Rouse, Linda P. (1988). Abuse in dating relationships: A comparison of Blacks, Whites, and Hispanics. *Journal of College Student Development,* Jul., v29 (4), 312-319.

Song, Young In (1986). Battered Korean women in urban America: The relationship of cultural conflict to wife abuse. *Dissertation Abstracts International,* Nov., v47 (5-A), 1,883.

Sue, Derald Wing and Sue, David (1990 rev.). *Counseling the culturally different: Theory and practice.* New York: Wiley Interscience.

Sue, Stanley and Nolan, Zane (1987). The role of culture and cultural techniques in psychotherapy: A critique and reformulation. *American Psychologist,* v2 (1), 37-45.

Takaki, Ronald (1993). *A different mirror: A history of multicultural America.* Boston: Little Brown and Company.

Tatum, Beverly Daniel (1992). Talking about race, learning about racism: The application of racial identity development theory in the classroom. *Harvard Educational Review,* v62 (1), 1-24.

Torres, Sara (1991). A comparison of wife abuse between two cultures: Perceptions, attitudes, nature, and extent. Special Issue: Psychiatric nursing for the 1990s: New concepts, new therapies. *Issues in Mental Health Nursing,* Jan.-Mar., v12 (1), 113-131.

Uzzell, Odell and Peebles-Wilkins, Wilma (1989). Black spouse abuse: A focus on relational factors and intervention strategies. *Western Journal of Black Studies,* Spring, v13 (1), 10-16.

LAW AND ETHICS, VIOLENCE AND DOMESTIC VIOLENCE

Bennett, Bruce E.; Bryant, Brenda K.; VandenBos, Gary R.; and Greenwood, Addison (1990). *Professional liability and risk management.* Washington, DC: American Psychological Association.

Brosig, Cheryl L. and Kalichman, Seth C. (1992). Clinicians' reporting of suspected child abuse: A review of the empirical literature. *Clinical Psychology Review,* 12 (n2), 155-168.

Campbell, Jacquelyn C. (ed.) (1994). *Assessing dangerousness: Violence by sexual offenders, batterers and child abusers.* Newbury Park, CA: Sage Publications, Inc.

Leslie, Richard S. (1989). Confidentiality. *The California Therapist.* The California Association of Marriage and Family Therapists Educational Foundation, July/August.

Leslie, Richard S. (1990). The dangerous patient: "Tarasoff" revisited. *The California Therapist.* The California Association of Marriage and Family Therapists Educational Foundation, March/April.

Leslie, Richard S. (1991). Psychotherapist-patient privilege clarified. *The California Therapist.* The California Association of Marriage and Family Therapists Educational Foundation, July/August.

Leslie, Richard S. (1991). Recent rulings shed light on "Tarasoff Warnings." *The California Therapist.* The California Association of Marriage and Family Therapists Educational Foundation, November/December.

Melton, Gary B. and Limber, Susan (1991). Caution in child maltreatment cases. *American Psychologist,* 46 (n1), 82-84.

Melton, Gary; Petrila, John; Poythress, Norman G.; and Slobogin, Christopher (1987). *Psychological evaluations for the courts: A handbook for mental health professionals and lawyers.* New York: Guilford Publications.

Monahan, John (ed.) (1980). *Who is the client: The ethics of psychological intervention in the criminal justice system.* Washington, DC: American Psychological Association.

Monahan, J. (1981). *Predicting violent behavior: An assessment of clinical techniques.* Beverly Hills, CA: Sage Publications, Inc.

Monahan, J. (1992). Mental disorder and violent behavior: Perceptions and evidence. *American Psychologist,* Apr., v47 (4), 511-521.

Monahan, J. (1993). Limiting therapist exposure to Tarasoff liability: Guidelines for risk containment. *American Psychologist,* Mar., v48 (3), 242-250.

Sonkin, Daniel Jay (1986). Clairvoyant vs. common sense: Therapist's duty to warn and protect. *Violence and Victims,* 1(1).

Sonkin, Daniel Jay and Ellison, Jean (1986). The therapist's duty to protect victims of domestic violence: Where we have been and where we are going. *Violence and Victims,* 1 (3).

Sonkin, Daniel and Liebert, Douglas (in press). Legal and ethical Issues in the treatment of multiple victimization of children. In: B. Rossman, M. Rosenberg, and R. Geffner (eds.), *Multiple victimization of children: Conceptual, developmental, research and treatment issues.* New York: Hawarth Press.

Order Form

____ **The Counselor's Guide to Learning to Live Without Violence** $29.95
by Daniel Jay Sonkin, Ph.D., hardcover

____ **Learning to Live Without Violence:** *A Handbook for Men* $13.95
by Daniel Jay Sonkin, Ph.D. and Michael Durphy, M.D.

____ **Learning to Live Without Violence:** *Worktape* $15.95
(2 C-60 cassettes)

____ **Family Violence and Religion:** *An Interfaith Resource Guide.* $29.95
Compiled by the Staff of Volcano Press, hardcover

____ **The Physician's Guide to Domestic Violence:** *How to ask* $10.95
the right questions and recognize abuse . . . another way to save a life
by Patricia R. Salber, M.D. and Ellen Taliaferro, M.D.

____ **Sourcebook for Working with Battered Women** $17.95
by Nancy Kilgore

____ **Every Eighteen Seconds:** *A Journey Through Domestic Violence* $8.95
by Nancy Kilgore

____ **Battered Wives** by Del Martin $12.95

____ **Conspiracy of Silence:** *The Trauma of Incest* $12.95
by Sandra Butler

____ **Menopause, Naturally:** *Preparing for the Second Half of Life,* $13.95
Updated, by Sadja Greenwood, M.D., M.P.H.

____ **Menopausia Sin Ansiedad.** Spanish edition of $13.95
Menopause, Naturally

____ **Period.** by JoAnn Gardner-Loulan, Bonnie Lopez and $9.95
Marcia Quackenbush

____ **La Menstruacion.** Spanish edition of *Period.* $9.95

____ **Lesbian/Woman** by Del Martin and Phyllis Lyon, hardcover $25.00

(continued on next page)

Youth and other titles from Volcano Press

____ **It's the Law!** *A Young Person's Guide to Our Legal System* $12.95
by Annette Carrel

____ **Facilitator's Guide to It's the Law!** by Annette Carrel $16.95

____ **African Animal Tales** by Rogério Andrade Barbosa, full $17.95
color, illustrated by Ciça Fittipaldi, translated by Feliz Guthrie

____ **Save My Rainforest** by Monica Zak, full color, illustrated $14.95
by Bengt-Arne Runnerström

____ **Berchick** by Esther Silverstein Blanc, illustrated by $14.95
Tennessee Dixon

____ **Mother Gave a Shout,** *Poems by Women and Girls* edited $14.95
by Susanna Steele and Morag Styles, illustrated by Jane Ray

____ **Mighty Mountain and the Three Strong Women,** full color, $14.95
hardcover, written and illustrated by Irene Hedlund

____ **Random Kindness & Senseless Acts of Beauty** by $14.95
Anne Herbert and Margaret Pavel with art by Mayumi Oda,
hardcover, accordion-fold

____ **People of the Noatak** by author/artist Claire Fejes $15.95

____ **Coit Tower:** *Its History & Art* by Masha Zakheim Jewett $10.00

____ **Goddesses** by Mayumi Oda, full color $14.95

To order directly, please send check or money order for the price of the book(s) plus $4.50 shipping and handling for the first book, and $1.00 for each additional book to Volcano Press, P.O. Box 270 SDV, Volcano, CA 95689. Order by phone with a VISA or MasterCard by calling toll-free, 1-800-VPWYMEN (1-800-879-9636).

California residents please add appropriate sales tax.

Volcano Press books are available at quantity discounts for bulk purchases, professional counseling, educational, fund-raising or premium use. Please call or write for details.

☐ Please send Volcano Press catalogs to:

Name: _____

Address: _____

City, State, Zip: _____